Liberalism

Pro and Con

A Primer

Stephen R. C. Hicks

CONNOR COURT PUBLISHING

Copyright © 2020, Stephen R. C. Hicks

ALL RIGHTS RESERVED. This book contains material protected under International and Federal Copyright Laws and Treaties. Any unauthorised reprint or use of this material is prohibited. No part of this book may be reproduced or transmitted in any form or by any means, electronic or mechanical, including photocopying, recording, or by any information storage and retrieval system without express written permission from the publisher.

CONNOR COURT PUBLISHING PTY LTD
PO Box 7257
Redland Bay QLD 4165
sales@connorcourt.com
www.connorcourt.com

Painting: Artist

Pere Borrell del Caso: Escaping Criticism (1874)

Collection Banco de España, Madrid, Wikipedia Commons.

ISBN: 978-1-925826-82-1 (pbk.)

Cover design by Maria Giordano

Printed in Australia

Contents

Foreword -- Parnell Palme McGuinness   1

Part One: The Stakes and the Method

1	What liberalism is	3
2	Why take up the strongest arguments?	5

Part Two: Fifteen Arguments for Liberalism

3	Liberalism increases freedom	9
4	People work harder in liberal societies	10
5	People work smarter under liberalism	11
6	Liberalism increases individuality and creativity	13
7	Liberalism increases the average standard of living	14
8	The poor are better off under liberalism	15
9	Liberalism generates more philanthropy	16
10	More outstanding individuals flourish under liberalism	17
11	Liberalism's individualism increases happiness	18
12	Liberal societies are more interesting	20
13	Tolerance increases under liberalism	22
14	Sexism and racism decrease under liberalism	23
15	Liberalism leads to international peace	25
16	Liberalism is the most just system	26
17	Liberalism is more moral in its political practice	28
18	Summary and Transition	30

Part Three: Fifteen Arguments against Liberalism

19	Humans are not intelligent enough for freedom	31
20	Human nature is too immoral for freedom	33
21	Liberalism is amorally self-interested	36
22	Liberalism's individualism is atomistic	37
23	Liberalism is materialistic	39
24	Liberal societies are boring	41
25	Power is the reality, so liberalism is naïve	43
26	Liberalism does not guarantee that everyone's basic needs will be met	45
27	Liberalism is unfair	46
28	Equality is threatened by freedom	48
29	Scarcity means that freedom is dog-eat-dog	51
30	Liberalism is unsustainable	53
31	Liberalism is socially inefficient	55
32	Liberalism is merely another subjective narrative	57
33	Freedom does not exist	61
34	Summary and Transition	63

Part Four: Conclusion—Arguments in Collision

35	Assessing the arguments for and against liberalism	65

Notes	68
Acknowledgments	106
About the Author	106

FOREWORD

Wouldn't it be nice if just for once the public figures making powerful arguments for their perspectives also acknowledged that there are equally persuasive points to be made on the other side? If, instead of arraigning arguments to bend our understanding to their perspective, they broadened our understanding, confident that our collective illumination will contribute to a more constructive overall debate. For, as the author of *Liberalism Pro and Con: A Primer* writes, "we make progress as individuals only when we know the most powerful arguments for and against what we judge to be true" and "we make progress socially only when we are able to articulate our views clearly... and when we ourselves genuinely understand what others think and why".

At the end of what Frances Fukiyama termed the end of history, the value and qualities of liberalism—finitely referred to as the "Liberal Project" or terminally as the "Liberal Experiment"—are again under examination. For students, Stephen R. C. Hicks' *Liberalism Pro and Con: A Primer* is a stepping stone into this grand philosophical question of our time, and a strong foundation from which to explore the matter. But the philosopher and the private intellectual will also benefit from the refreshing reset the *Primer* provides. No one is educated who knows only one side of the argument, writes Hicks, quoting John Stuart Mill. And even the most sophisticated thinker can benefit from re-encountering and re-examining the fundamental ideas on which her elaborations are based.

The *Primer* employs the philosophical *principle of charity* to lay out the arguments for and against liberalism, presenting the strongest, clearest and most credible argument for each perspective, generously footnoted with quotes and attributions to philosophers and intellectuals who have held these views. The clarity and simplicity with which Hicks lays out the arguments serves to highlight their potential flaws, without insisting on them.

The *Primer* can be used in a number of different ways, and I would encourage multiple readings. For a start, I recommend reading it without referring to the footnotes to appreciate the arguments free of the ideological dead hand of past heroes. Then read just the footnotes to uncover the unexpected alignments of thought among these great figures of history, from Karl Marx to Roger Scruton, many of whom are taught as opposite political poles.

Finally, the *Primer* is a reading guide for further immersion into the topic, as every quote suggests another line of enquiry and encourages the reader to visit or revisit the works of the original author.

What comes of that appointment is up to you.

-- Parnell Palme McGuinness

1

The Stakes and the Method

1

What liberalism is. The major political issue of the modern era is the fate of liberalism. Liberalism is a newcomer to human history, after millennia of tribalism, feudalism, and many types of dictatorship. Liberalism had a few short-lived successes in classical Greece and Rome and more recently in some Renaissance Italian and Baltic states. Only in the past few centuries has liberalism become a prevailing theory and practice, and only in some parts of the world. It is a work in progress and, aside from resistance from traditional forms of politics, it faces formidable practical and theoretical opposition from other political newcomers such as modern communalism, fascism, updated military dictatorship, and systems that try to mix them in some combination.

Whether liberalism is viable is an open question.

By *liberalism* I mean the social system that makes foundational the liberty of the individual in all areas of life—artistic, religious, economic, sexual, political, and so on.[1]

The question of the proper role of government within a social system is central to any political theory. A government is a social institution distinguished by two traits: its principles apply to the whole of society and they are enacted by physical force or its threat. Governments claim and practice *universality* and *compulsion*.

In these two respects government is distinguished from other social institutions, such as businesses, religious associations, sports teams, and so on, which are *particular* and *voluntary*. Not everyone in a society does business with a given company, joins a given church, temple, or mosque, or plays a given sport. When a member disagrees with or breaks one of those institutions' rules, the most that the institution can do is dissociate itself from that member.

A government, by contrast, claims and enacts the authority to apply its rules to everyone in a society, and it claims and enacts the authority to use physical force against those who break its rules. It is a universal institution of compulsion.

Consequently, the two key questions to answer when defining the proper, principled role of government are: What principles are so important that *everyone* in society should respect and live by them? What principles are so important that *physical force* may be used against those who violate them?

The liberal answer to both of those questions is, of course, liberty. All individuals are entitled to liberty and all individuals should respect each other's freedoms. That is the universality element. Any individual who violates the liberty of another can properly be subject to physical force. That is the compulsion element.

To protect freedoms, liberal societies devise a network of institutional elements. They specify religious liberties, property rights, free-speech rights, liberties to engage in commercial activities, and more. They set up police, courts, and prisons to investigate those who violate others' freedoms and to restrain those guilty of doing so. They place limitations on the scope and power of government in order to lessen the risk that government itself will violate liberties. They articulate a commitment to the rule of law by making their general principles explicit in a constitution and devising their particular rules by reference to those general principles.

All of that follows from making liberty the foundational political value. Advocates of other systems disagree, and the debate is engaged. Is liberty really the *most* important social value? What about security, equality, justice, peace, efficiency, prosperity, or spiritual purity? Is liberty *compatible* with them, and if so, how? Or if it is in tension with them, why *prioritize* liberty?

2

Why take up the strongest arguments? In this primer, our method starts by taking up the best arguments for and against liberalism. I make fifteen arguments for liberalism and fifteen against. These fifteen arguments on opposite sides of the debate are not exhaustive, but they include those that have had the most staying power over the long history of argument and counter-argument about liberalism. The reason they have had that staying power is that each identifies and stresses a genuinely important value at stake in politics.

John Stuart Mill, in *On Liberty*, best expresses the reason for using a for-and-against method.[2] No one is educated who knows only one side of an argument. No one should commit to a position without knowing the position's competition. Especially in complicated matters like politics, where a huge number of facts about the world must be integrated into a theory, a critical test for any theory is how well it compares with other theories. Does it overlook key facts? Does it make leaps of logic? The best way to answer for oneself those questions is to put the contender theories, with reference to their strongest defenders, in explicit competition with each other.

An advocate of liberalism has to know not only the best arguments for liberalism but also the best arguments against liberalism—and how to respond to them. An opponent of liberalism must also know the best arguments for liberalism—and how to respond to them.

As author of this primer, my views on liberalism should not matter. So my first goal will be to rise to Mill's challenge. After presenting arguments for liberalism, with reference to their strongest advocates,

I will present the arguments against liberalism in their strongest form, with reference to their strongest advocates. Liberalism has many intelligent, decent, and articulate enemies, and their qualms and fears about liberalism must be taken seriously. Liberalism has many equally intelligent, decent, and articulate advocates, and their enthusiasm and endorsements of liberalism must also be taken seriously.

One test of success of this primer will be this: Could a reader who read only its presentation of the arguments for and against liberalism tell which side of the debate I am on?

We make progress as individuals only when we know the most powerful arguments for and against what we judge to be true, and we can best judge the truth of a position by testing it against its worthy competitors. We often want shortcuts, perhaps out of intellectual laziness, an unwillingness to admit errors, or to protect some belief we feel is core to our identity. But there are no shortcuts on complicated matters.

We make progress socially only when we are able to articulate our views clearly to others who are trying to understand—and when we ourselves genuinely understand what others think and why. We often talk past each other, and discussion degenerates when one party senses that the other isn't really listening or is addressing a weaker, easily attackable version of one's position.

The next step is to compare the two sets of arguments. Where are the sharpest and most persistent disagreements between liberals and their opponents? Some disagreements turn on issues within economics (e.g., Do free markets lead to monopoly?)—within politics (e.g., Was the American Revolution ideologically conservative or libertarian?)—or about history (e.g., Were the British Acts of Toleration primarily about religion?), and so on.

But many significant differences between liberals and their opponents are driven by disagreements in philosophy. That is, disagreements about values, human nature, metaphysics, and epistemology drive deep and protracted arguments about politics.

Consider this claim, for example: *Free societies may be practically efficient at generating wealth, but they are not moral.* That raises issues of ethics: What conception of morality is at work here, and why is it opposed to the practical? Or consider the opposite claim: *Liberalism is a fine ideal, but it's unrealistic to expect it actually to work in the real world.* That raises a set of metaphysical concerns: What is the real world, where do ideals come from, and why are fine ideals not realistic?

Or one can challenge my method sketched above: *This arguments-back-and-forth procedure—isn't that pointless given human psychology? Don't studies show that people reject or accept empirical data for or against a policy depending on their prior commitments? So what is the point of reasoning?*

This challenge illustrates the importance of epistemology. Political arguments often turn on philosophical assumptions about cognition: Are humans rational or irrational? Or if a mix, what level of rational competency can we expect from them? If we are devising a set of political principles for human beings, then they must be based on an accurate understanding of human nature, which must include an accurate understanding of our cognitive powers. Those with dramatically different epistemologies are almost always led to very different politics, and they advocate them by very different methods.

Historically, philosophy is the mother discipline, giving birth to the specific sciences and nurturing them to maturity. But the point about the importance of philosophy is not to assert a professional monopoly on philosophy by professional philosophers. Everyone is philosophical to some extent, and we are necessarily philosophical when we think about social theory, whether we do so as professional economists, political scientists, historians, or voting citizens. Philosophy is a practice common to all thinking human beings.

Explicit attention to the philosophical issues embedded within any political theory is necessary for understanding, defending, or attacking that theory competently. The value-added by professional philosophers is part of an overall intellectual division of labor. Economists, political theorists, historians, and others all have specialties that contribute the knowledge necessary to a comprehensive social theory, but labor that has been divided also must be coordinated again. That coordinating work of integrating knowledge from various disciplines is a task that each of us must perform individually. No one can do social theory adequately without being also an economist, a political theorist, a historian—and, especially, a philosopher.

Now for the arguments for and against liberalism. I will present them in qualitative form and keep the scholarly apparatus to a minimum by putting in the footnotes relevant quotations from major thinkers who make points supporting or illustrating the argument in question. The footnotes may be useful for those interested in the historically important thinkers who have contributed to the debate. But they can be ignored by those interested primarily in focusing quickly on the arguments' essential points and putting them in collision with each other.

2

Fifteen Arguments for Liberalism

3

Liberalism increases freedom. Liberalism dramatically increases the amount of *freedom* that individuals enjoy relative to any other kind of society that can be devised: monarchy, socialism, fascism, tribalism, and the rest. Under the liberal set of institutions—the specification of individual rights, limited government, rule of law—individuals enjoy more freedom because those institutions expressly make liberty their core purpose.

Most of us like the exercise of freedom. We like to do things our own way, to formulate our own tastes, to dream our dreams, and to be able to put them into practice.

But liberals also argue that freedom is not only something that we happen to like. There is a deep *need* within human nature to be who we are by our own making.[3] To live a fully human life, we each need to decide our own careers, choose our own romantic partners, formulate our own musical tastes, and chart our own courses in the world. We are each unique as individuals in our specific traits and needs—but we are also the same in needing the freedom to discover and create our individuality. Liberty is a fundamental human value.

Therefore, a society that respects and augments the amount of freedom that individuals enjoy is, by that criterion alone, a good society. Human beings are not slaves; they are not even servants.

Every human is by nature a free, autonomous individual, and one proper purpose of society is to protect individuals' freedom.

4

People work harder in liberal societies. Suppose that we have a society in which the freedom of thought and action, property rights, and so forth are protected. Economists and psychologists argue that in such a liberal system individuals' *incentive to work hard* changes for the positive.

If I am able to do what I want, choose who I want to be, and make a living the way that I want to—and if I know that I will be able to keep the fruits of my labor—then I am more likely to exert myself to achieve my goals. Most individuals in a liberal society will work hard and, as a result, they will produce a lot of economic value. Consequently, that society will prosper economically.

Compare liberalism to other political systems. Under *tribalism*, I am supposed to work primarily for the good of the tribe. If I am raised in that tribe, I will have some incentive, of course, to work for its advancement. Or under *feudalism*: I am required to work for the aristocrats, the clergy, and the other castes. Even if I am a serf, I will likely feel some motivation to support the lifestyle of my betters. Another possibility is *socialism*, where I am supposed to work selflessly for the collective good of society. To the extent that I value those institutions—tribal, feudal, socialist—I will have an incentive to exert myself on their behalf.

However, liberals argue, to the extent that I am able to work for myself and keep the fruits of my own labor, I will consistently work harder. I will become a carpenter or an artist or a scientist because I want to, not because I have been ordered or pressured into that career by social regulation. I will also know that the rewards, both material and psychological, for being an excellent carpenter, artist, or scientist will be mine to keep.

Liberal societies, therefore, will be more prosperous than other kinds of societies.[4]

5

People work smarter under liberalism. A complementary argument is that under liberalism not only do people work harder, they work *smarter*. The most important asset in any economy is knowledge, and liberalism makes the best use of the knowledge available in a society. In any society, knowledge is dispersed among the minds of its many individuals—thousands, millions, or billions of individuals know uncountably many things. Liberalism enables those individuals to act on their knowledge, instead of having to follow orders or wait for permission. And liberalism develops institutions—such as free markets with their supply-and-demand price systems—that enable those individuals to mobilize and coordinate their knowledge in a way better than in any other society.

Contrast a monarchy, for example. Suppose that we have a king trying to organize and run a whole economy. The king might be hard-working and he might be very smart. (How many kings possess both of those traits, though?[5]) Nonetheless, there is a limit to how much one person can know, and the king can necessarily make only crude, top-down decisions in a centralized fashion. How much corn should be raised? How many soldiers should be recruited? How many musical concerts organized? What should the price of cloth be? And so on, for thousands of other economic matters. There is a severe limit to how much one king can know about these matters and, consequently, there is a severe limit to how productive a monarchy's economy can be.

Consider a socialist planning board, for another example. The socialist central-planning committee might be made up of ten or twenty well-meaning, intelligent individuals who jointly make decisions for an economy as a whole. Nonetheless, there is a limit to how much even ten or twenty people can know, and there is a limit to the quantity and quality of the decisions they can make for society as a whole. If each major decision is allotted, say, an hour's worth of investigation and thought, then only a dozen or so major decisions can be made in a day. How many other important and semi-important decisions simply will not be made? And how many of the actual decisions will be best, given that they were reached after only an hour's deliberation?

By contrast, liberalism is characterized by decentralized decision-making. Liberalism enables each individual to think and act as he or she judges best. In a society of millions of individuals, there are millions who are free to make their own decisions in their own life. Each of those decision-makers is much more likely to know his or her needs and circumstances better than a king or a central-planning committee does. Thus, free individuals are better positioned to decide what they need to do and to decide what relationships with other people will work best to satisfy their needs.

That is to say, free, decentralized systems better utilize the knowledge available in society. Millions of people know more than a few do, and the local knowledge of each of those millions is usually more accurate. So liberalism's freedom enables individuals to act on their knowledge of what is necessary for their particular circumstances in a more productive way than any other kind of system.[6]

The better use of knowledge extends to the more impersonal markets that liberalism develops. In stock, commodity, and financial markets, prices capture information about what each individual, from his or her unique situation, is willing to sell or buy for. Those supply-and-demand prices send signals to other individuals around the world, enabling them to decide better how to use the resources available to them. If there is a greater need for iron in Brazil than in Finland, for example, then that will be communicated by Brazilians' willingness to pay more for iron. If there is a greater supply of iron available in Canada than in Japan, then that will be reflected in Canadians' willingness to sell their iron for less. The prevailing prices will lead Canadians and Brazilians to be more likely to buy and sell iron with each other, and that will be the most optimal result. The price system thus efficiently coordinates the decision-making of all participants.[7]

Free-market systems thus work smarter and, as a result of working smarter, they become more prosperous.

6

Liberalism increases individuality and creativity. Another complementary argument about the greater economic productivity of liberalism is that, in a liberal society, people have more freedom to live their lives as they want. Liberal societies are therefore characterized by an increased amount of *individuality*—that is, a greater number of people who do their own thing in their own way. They are free to adopt the lifestyles they want, to think the thoughts that they want, to experiment however they want.

As a result, liberal societies are more *creative* societies. Creativity is a function of free thinking, experimentalism, a willingness to take risks, and a social system that protects and encourages individuals who do so.[8] As a result of that increased creativity, there will be more *innovation* in liberal societies compared to other kinds of societies.

Other societies, by contrast—if they prize everybody doing the same thing in the same way, or if they prize everybody following orders—will not cultivate the creativity and innovation that happens in liberal societies.

As a result of liberalism's creativity and innovation, such societies will be dynamic and progressive. They will produce more free-thinking scientists, more experimental engineers, and more creative business professionals trying to satisfy the demands of more customers who want unique goods and services to fit their individual lifestyles. Consequently, liberal societies will be more prosperous.⁹

To integrate the previous three arguments: Under liberalism—which increases the amount of freedom that people have in that society—people will work *harder*, *smarter*, and more *creatively*. That is why liberal societies produce much more wealth than any other kind of society can.

7

Liberalism increases the average standard of living. The next arguments focus not on liberalism's *productive* ability or how much wealth it creates, but instead on the *distribution* of wealth in a society.

One characteristic of liberalism in the modern world, after the Industrial Revolution especially, was the mass production of goods: clothing, food, houses, cars, televisions, and more. By dramatically increasing the *quantity* of goods produced, the *cost* to consumers of those goods correspondingly declined dramatically. More people became able to enjoy more goods at lower cost. Consequently, the *average* standard of living increased.

Compare the more free-market societies to monarchies, socialist societies, fascist societies, and tribal societies. All of them have demonstrably lower average standards of living, and the majority of their people live less well than in liberal societies.

A closely related argument is that the *quality* of goods increased after the Industrial Revolution. Humans get tired, they can be unmotivated and sloppy, and they have physical limits—their visual acuity and their manual dexterity, for example. But ingenious science and engineering can devise machines that work more precisely and consistently, so the overall quality of goods increases. Machines are often able to operate at a larger or smaller physical scale than humans can, so the quality of very large and very small goods increases.

As a result, in liberal societies, consumers enjoy more goods, better-quality goods, and at lower prices.

So, if one's measure of a good society is increasing the *average* standard of living or increasing the standard of living enjoyed by the *majority* of people in the society, then liberalism performs better than any other society.[10]

8

The poor are better off under liberalism. Rather than focusing on the middle class, the average, or the majority of people in a society—we can focus on the *poorest* people in society and consider liberalism's effects on them.

The liberal argument here is that because free-market societies produce a great deal of wealth, those societies are best able to help the least well-off economically.[11] In prosperous societies, a significant amount of the wealth generated will be reinvested in new productive enterprises, and that reinvestment will create more jobs. Additionally, those jobs will typically be better paid as a result of the increase in overall standard of living in that society.

Also, with liberalism, poor individuals have more freedom to become entrepreneurs, so as to improve their condition and, hopefully, work their way out of poverty. They are not prevented from doing so by tribal restrictions, by their place in the feudal hierarchy, or by the mandates of a socialist planning committee.

The argument of the previous section carries over: As the quantity, cost, and quality of goods in liberal societies improves, the poor—as consumers—also have access to more goods, at lower cost, and of higher quality.

Liberalism thus improves the lot of poorer people by encouraging entrepreneurial effort for those who wish to do so, by increasing the number of job opportunities for those who prefer to work for an existing business, and by improving their lot as consumers.

This argument is borne out historically by looking at the number of people living under the poverty line. If we keep the poverty line consistent, the vast majority of people who lived in poverty were lifted out of poverty as liberalism developed, until poverty in the advanced liberal societies became a relatively minor issue.[12]

To put the argument pointedly: One would prefer being poor in a liberal society to being poor in any other kind of society.

9

Liberalism generates more philanthropy. Another, related argument focuses on the philanthropic sector under liberalism. Liberal societies produce much wealth, and much of that wealth is spent directly on consumer goods or reinvested in new productive enterprises.

Much of that wealth, though, will be directed to philanthropic organizations, including research institutions that are devoted to studying cures for new diseases, charity hospitals, disaster-response organizations, cultural associations, education programs, and agencies that support the handicapped who cannot support themselves.

Liberalism, in other words, generates a more robust civil society compared to any other kind of society.

The argument is partly that the material prosperity of liberal societies means that more wealth is available for philanthropy. It is also partly that prosperity increases and extends our natural benevolence. Once one's own material needs are looked after—once life is no longer a desperate matter of day-to-day survival—one is both materially able and psychologically freer to expand the range of one's thinking and action. One can think of individuals in more distant places and one has the resources available to reach them. One can think longer-term about the future and invest in it. Benevolence is more possible and more easily extended to others in prosperous societies.

Furthermore: Liberalism is a do-it-yourself society. Its cultural ethos emphasizes self-responsibility and expects that individuals will show initiative in solving problems, marshaling the necessary resources, and developing social institutions. It does not, as other systems do, shift that responsibility to aristocrats or government agencies and expect citizens more passively to follow their lead. Consequently, for any type of social goal, including philanthropic goals, under liberalism more initiatives are undertaken in more directions, and the energies of more people are mobilized.[13]

Liberal societies, therefore, are *more* philanthropic and often at a *higher rate*.

Again to put the argument pointedly: If you're a sick person who has no resources, or if you're a handicapped person and not able to support yourself, then you want to be in a liberal society because that will most increase your chances of getting the resources you need to deal with your difficult situation.

10

More outstanding individuals flourish under liberalism. Here is another complementary argument in the area of *distribution*.

Rather than focusing on the average person, the poor person, or the person who is so weak and handicapped that he or she can't support himself, we also consider the effects of liberalism's wealth on the most *able* people, the most *intelligent* people, the people who are the *creative* geniuses in the arts, the *outstanding* athletes, and the people who are the *innovative* intellectuals or scientists.

Most of those individuals need huge amounts of resources. The sciences, for example, are wealth-intensive disciplines, given the high cost of educating a scientist to the forefront of his or her area of expertise and the cost of equipping and stocking a research laboratory. Great artists need much leisure time, education, and often travel in order to be able to do what they do. The production of a first-rate movie, for example, requires the talent of hundreds of creative professionals. Symphony orchestras, as another example, are obviously very wealth-intensive—to be able to put together a whole orchestra costs a lot of money. Or even to take a four-member rock-and-roll band on the road requires considerable resources. The best athletes need practice time, coaches, equipment, specialized nutrition and medical care, and often the ability to travel abroad to compete against the world's best.

All such people—those who are the most outstanding in the sciences, the arts, athletics, and so forth—will flourish more in a liberal society. There will be more individuals enabled to reach their highest potential. The rest of us will be able to enjoy more of what they are able to accomplish, precisely because liberalism is able to generate the wealth to empower them to do the awesome things that they do.[14]

Such individuals also need the freedom to think and feel independently and to experiment. Any system, by contrast, that encourages conformity or obedience and enforces such traits by fear undercuts human development. By recognizing the need for freedom as fundamental to being human, liberalism establishes the conditions necessary for more individuals to reach their fullest potentials.[15]

11

Liberalism's individualism increases happiness. By protecting the amount of freedom that individuals enjoy, liberal societies cultivate and encourage individuality—and that means we will have more *happy* people in society. Individuals are happiest when they do their own things in their own way. Most of us resent being told what to do, being made to do things that we don't want to do, and not being able to enjoy the fruits of our labor. Those are all affronts to our individuality.

More formally, the argument is happiness is *conditional*. Individuals must (1) define their own values and goals, (2) show initiative and exert themselves, and, of course, (3) achieve their goals. Life is also complicated; happiness typically requires success in a wide range of life activities—career, friendships, romance, family, leisure activities, self-assessment, and wisdom. And happiness is most fully experienced when an individual is able to say, with the given emphases: I *chose* that goal. I *made* it happen. And I *succeeded*.

Liberals encourage people to define their own major life goals and to develop their own tastes, rather than, as other systems do, expect or require them to live as others have decided.[16] Liberal systems do not assign individuals to jobs—they let them choose whatever career they want to go into. Liberals do not select others' marriage partners for them or tell them how many children they may have, or even make them get married. Beyond career and marriage, liberals encourage people to cultivate their own musical likes, develop their own fashion style, watch whatever movies, and read whatever books they want. People can, of course, sometimes find satisfaction in doing work they are ordered to do, in arranged marriages, and in the books chosen for them by others. But more people will find more pleasures in values they've chosen for themselves.

Furthermore, happiness is earned and not given to anyone.[17] A dollar earned is more satisfying than a dollar received as allowance from one's parents. A student who works hard for a grade feels more happiness than a student who cheats. A recorded win in sports is more rewarding if it results from sweaty effort than if it results from one's opponent having defaulted. A house brings pleasure, but a house you designed or furnished yourself brings more. Liberalism emphasizes individual initiative and the expectation that accomplishment in life is primarily up to each individual. Liberalism thus argues that other social systems *undermine* happiness by teaching them that life's needs and wants are to be provided for by the tribe, the reciprocal fulfillment of the duties of feudal castes to each other, or the obligatory, collective exertions of society as a whole.

Happiness also requires actual success. It is difficult to be happy when your career is in the toilet, your marriage is failing, you have a serious disease, your children despise you, and/or you are bored by life in general. Any one of those challenges can put one in a depressive state. And certainly, in a liberal society that emphasizes freedom and self-responsibility, there are many risks. Some books make you sad, some romances end in disaster, some careers reach dead-ends, and some family members make us miserable. But, liberalism argues, success is more likely in life endeavors that you have chosen yourself and when you believe that success or failure is primarily up to you.

All of this ties into liberalism's argument that liberalism is more productive and so leads to a wealthier society. Money, contrary to cliché, *does* buy many of the ingredients of happiness. The preconditions of successful action—education, health, resources for starting a business, and so on—can be expensive. Prosperity also makes it easier for parents to encourage their children to define themselves and their own goals. It makes it easier for individuals to embrace riskier choices if they have a financial cushion in case of failure. Prosperity of course provides the material resources for people to try a wider range of happiness-generating activities.

By contrast, non-liberal societies—either by ordering people to live a certain way, by not allowing them to do what they want, by assigning them to jobs, by taking the fruits of their labor away from them, or simply by not enabling them to reach their economic potential—such societies undercut or actively discourage happiness and increase the amount of misery.

Liberal societies encourage individuality in all areas of life. It is precisely through being our own person, living our own lives our own way, meeting challenges, and accomplishing our goals that we become happy and fulfilled individuals.[18]

12

Liberal societies are more interesting. By encouraging individuality in society, the next argument is that liberal societies are *more interesting* societies. This is an aesthetic criterion of value.

Consider what makes going to parties interesting, or what makes travelling to new parts of the world interesting. We are interested in people doing things *differently*, people being *unique* and *authentic* in their own way.

What we find in liberal societies, precisely because of their liberality, is more people doing their own thing and pursuing their own life adventures. Liberal societies will have many eccentric people, of course, some charming and some not, but many of those eccentrics will be intriguing in their own right and many will do interesting things in the arts, the sciences, philosophy, business, and other walks of life.[19]

Other societies, by contrast, place other values above liberty and thus direct the character of their cultures in different directions. In monarchies, aristocracies, dictatorships, and other sorts of authoritarian societies, the top political value is *obedience* to those further up the hierarchy. Obedient people are not those who think and act for themselves; they follow the rules. In socialism, communism, fascism, and other collectivistic societies, the top political value is *communalism*. Communal people do not think and act independently;

rather, they strive for sameness of purpose and action.

Liberalism enables and encourages lifestyle diversity, and such diversity gives all of us more social options. We can choose to live among people who share our tastes and styles, of course, or we can choose to seek out the exotic and unique.

The argument about the greater wealth of liberal societies works with this aesthetic criterion. Liberalism encourages individuality and its consequent diversity, but it also generates the wealth to enable individualized pursuits. A liberal society will be able to support a wider diversity of restaurants catering to different food tastes, more musical types of experimental and traditional music, more museums of art and history, and more travel to exotic places. By increasing mass production, it will enable more people to enjoy more diverse goods and services. And by supporting smaller niche markets, it will enable those with specialized tastes to satisfy their preferences.

Liberal societies, then, will have more interesting people and more varied activities, with more individuals pursuing their own unique life adventures, and they will be a lot more fun to live in—in contrast to societies that are more conformist or driven by hierarchy or obedience.

13

Tolerance increases under liberalism. Liberal societies are *tolerant* societies. Consider religious intolerance, for example, a social ill that has plagued human beings for as long as there has been religion. It is precisely in societies that have encouraged individual freedom—that is, that believe that individuals should be free to live their lives as they see fit, encourage individuality, emphasize the importance of each individual deciding for himself or herself what he thinks is true or important, and what he or she is going to do with respect to religious matters[20]—that we see the rise of religious tolerance.[21]

If you and I both believe, as a matter of principle, that people should be free to live their lives as they see fit, including in their religious practices, then I will respect your liberty to practice religion as you choose, I will jealously guard my right to live my religious life as I choose, and you will do the same. To the extent that we also have liberal political institutions protecting religious freedoms, a more tolerant society will result.

Under liberalism, the principle of toleration of individuals' free choices in religious matters also extends to government actions, meaning that government officers are prohibited from using their political power either to endorse or suppress religion. The principle of the separation of church and state, as it is colloquially called, is more generally a separation of religion from politics.[22] Contrary to the doctrines of *theocratic* political theories such as Islamism, the state's mandating of particular religious beliefs or practices is not allowed under liberalism. And contrary to the doctrines of *atheistic* political theories such as Marxism, the state's abolishing of religious belief or practice is not allowed. Consequently, by keeping the state's great power out of religion, liberalism tames one traditionally powerful source of religious intolerance.

14

Sexism and racism decrease under liberalism. Liberalism leads to a decrease in racism and sexism. Since the general principles of life, liberty, and property rights are human rights, and individuals of both sexes and all races are human beings, liberalism argues that traditional sexism and racism are affronts to liberal individualism.

Racism and sexism have been prominent features of cultures all over the world for millennia. It is not coincidental, liberals argue, that for the first time in history racism and sexism were challenged and put on the defensive precisely in those societies that took individuality and liberty seriously. Liberal societies were and will be at the forefront of eliminating traditional racism and sexism.[23]

Liberalism's free market provides further incentives against sexism and racism. We can see this with respect to profit motive, for example, which is a prominent feature of a free-market economy. Suppose that I am in business and I want to make a lot of money. That is the profit motive. Suppose also, though, that I am a traditional sexist, and I am hiring. I have two candidates available. One is a young woman, who just graduated from university with **A** grades; the other is a young man who just graduated from university with **C** grades.

Whom will I hire? The sexist in me will say: "I want to hire the male, not the female." But the profit-seeking liberal in me will say, "Definitely, I will hire the female, because she is smarter and works harder, and she is the one who is going to enable me to make more money."

So, this argument concludes, liberalism's encouragement of the profit motive will lead people to be more likely to set aside traditional sexist attitudes. As a result, more men and women will work with each other and the sexist attitudes will decline.

The same pattern holds for racism. Suppose that I am a profit-seeker in a free market, but I am also a traditional racist. I am, say, a white person who does not like to work with brown people. But suppose I have a brown customer who comes to me and says that he wants to buy $100,000 worth of goods from me. The profit-seeker in me will say, "I want that $100,000 in sales." The traditional racist in me will say, "I don't like dealing with brown people." Which desire will override? How high a price am I willing to pay for my racism?

The argument is that the profit motive gives everyone an incentive to set aside racial differences and to deal peacefully in a win-win fashion with people of other races. Once people start to do that, traditional racial attitudes decline.[24]

The same pattern of argument applies to ethnic differences. Liberals argue that traditional national or cultural enemies will come to at least tolerate each other as the principles of respect for individual liberty and the prospects for win-win trade become prevalent.

15

Liberalism leads to international peace. Liberalism makes fundamental respect for other individuals' freedoms and their property rights. Many wars in history, though, have been motivated by the desire to control others' lives or to confiscate their wealth. Liberalism argues that those two motives are illegitimate, and so it offers a principled opposition to them as reasons for war.

Beyond that, the profit motive also powerfully incentivizes peace. Liberalism leads to much trade, including free trade across regional and international borders. Globalization is one of the major trends of the liberal era. If I am dealing with people in other countries, they are my suppliers and my customers, so I do not want to go to war with them. If foreigners are buying millions of dollars' worth of my goods each year, then I do not want them killed. I do not want disrupted the trade networks that are putting money in my pocket.

The same reasoning holds if my suppliers are from another country. I want them to continue to send the raw materials that I need to make whatever I am producing. I do not want my country to go to war with their country, because I do not want my suppliers killed or have their factories bombed or have them forbidden to trade with me. Doing so will undermine my ability to make money.[25]

Liberalism fosters trading relationships among nations, and those trading relationships give people an incentive to remain at peace with each other.

16

Liberalism is the most just system. Justice is the application of a moral standard to our individual practices and social institutions and their outcomes.[26] The claim of liberalism as a political system is based on a unique and prior moral claim about what individuals deserve. That prior claim is that, fundamentally, individuals make or break their own lives. The good things in life—the material means of survival, a satisfying career, a rewarding inner life, meaningful friendships—must be achieved. Value, in other words, has to be created, and those who create value should be rewarded in proportion to the value they create.

In yet more abstract words, justice is the principle of cause and effect applied to human action. If by my actions I cause good, then the consequential effect should be that I am rewarded. If I *produce* something of economic value (e.g., knitting a hat or building a house), then I deserve the use of it. If by *trade* I bring value to others (e.g., by bringing wheat or software to market), then I deserve the wealth that I receive from my customers. If I *develop* my intellect and emotions, then I deserve the rewards of a cultivated psychological life. If by my personality and character I *add richness* to others' lives, then I deserve the rewards of friendship and love.[27]

The negatives of cause and effect also hold. If I simply fail to produce or trade or develop myself, then it is sadly appropriate that I will be poor, lonely, and not even like my own company. And if I actively cause destruction in my life or in others', then I deserve to bear the costs—the self-loathing and the active dislike and punishment that others will inflict upon me.

Injustice is the opposite—the *severing* of cause and effect in human action. If you bake bread and I throw it in the trash, if you write an essay and I plagiarize it, or if you commit a good deed and I withhold praise, then all of those are acts of injustice. In each case I sever the enjoyment of the effect from its enabling cause. If you steal from others, assault them, or spread malicious gossip about them—and I *praise* you for doing so—then I commit injustice by failing to judge you negatively for your destructive actions.

Individuals and institutions are just to the extent that they *evaluate* themselves and others according to what they deserve and *act* on those evaluations.

Liberals then argue that liberal institutions are most just in four respects.

(1) In a society based on self-responsibility and freedom, more individuals will end up in life circumstances that are the result of their own choices and efforts. Most people will get what they deserve.

(2) Socially, individuals in a liberal society are taught to evaluate themselves and others according to their character and accomplishments as individuals. Liberal culture, therefore, is more respectful and admiring of achievement and, correspondingly, more disrespectful of laziness and destruction.

(3) Economically, the wealth that individuals acquire will only be from production and voluntary trade or gifts from others. In a system of property rights, individuals get to keep the fruits of their labor and of their trade with others. In a free market, trade occurs according to the value that each participant thinks others are providing to them. In any trade, the individuals involved are the best judges of the value that each is offering the other. Thus, the amount of wealth that individuals acquire as a result of free actions is the best estimate possible of the value they have added to their own lives and the lives of others.

(4) Legally, a liberal system is committed to making laws that protect individual freedoms. It creates the largest social space possible for its citizens to make their own choices and to live with the consequences. A liberal legal system also dedicates itself to handling those who do not respect others' freedoms. It exerts itself to prevent injustices, and, when injustices occur, it attempts to measure accurately the

degree of destructiveness they caused and the appropriate amount of compensation owed.[28] It does so by explicit, constitutionally specified procedures that limit the power of government to prevent government itself from becoming a source of injustice.[29]

Other political systems, by contrast, undercut justice by wanting causes without effects and effects without causes.

In feudal institutions, for example, individuals do not earn their social status by their own productive efforts. Rather, their place in the hierarchy is acquired by irrelevant-to-justice considerations such as conquest or accident of birth. Once the hierarchy is established, individuals within it receive goods out of proportion to the value they add. The peasants, for example, receive a fraction of the economic value of the goods they produce, while the aristocrats receive far more. Thus, feudalism institutionalizes unjust initial status and unjust consequent distribution.

The same is true of socialism. Socialist governments assert ownership over all of their citizens and require them to work on government-approved projects. Individuals have their uniqueness and energy taken from them by an irrelevant-to-justice consideration—the desire of some people to control the lives of others. According to socialism's principle of equality-of-outcome, goods are to be distributed equally among the citizens. Those who are more productive will receive the same amount as those who are less productive. Thus, socialism also institutionalizes unjust initial status and unjust consequent distribution.

17

Liberalism is more moral in its political practice. Under liberalism, political power is granted only for the purpose of protecting individuals' rights to live their own lives freely—to make their own livings, interact with others voluntarily, and keep the rewards of their efforts.

Other political systems, by contrast, increase the scope of government power. Some want the government to regulate the economy, people's diets, sex lives, religious practices, or artistic pursuits. All such systems, accordingly, increase the potential for the corrupt use of political power. If the government regulates business practice, then that puts large amounts of money under government control, and that increases incentives and opportunities for bribery, nepotism, kickbacks, and other forms of financial corruption. If government has power over legitimate artistic, sexual, or religious activities, then all of those powers are political weapons that can be used against some and in favor of others. Also, more individuals are attracted to government offices who want to have power over others and who are willing to use that power for the corrupt opportunities it makes possible.

Liberals argue, by contrast, that the responsibility for our economic, sex, dietary, religious, and artistic affairs lies with each individual, so it does not grant government officials power over them. It therefore advocates a series of principled separations—the separation of state from religion, the economy, our sex lives, our artistic pursuits, and so on. Such limitations on the proper scope of political power thus lessen the scope of political corruption. The political power that government officials have under liberalism will of course sometimes be abused, but abuse is less possible than in other systems.

Governments have more power than any other social institution, because they have the power of the police and the military at their direct disposal and the authority to apply that power to every member of society. Consequently, the worst abuses in history—wars, democide,[30] the legalizing and enforcing of slavery, the confiscation of property, and more—have been caused by governments. Private individuals and organizations can of course kill, kidnap, and steal from each other, but their power to do so is much less than that of a government. So a political system that places explicit limits on the power of government and enforces those limits vigilantly, as liberalism strives to do, is in practice a more moral system.

18

Summary and Transition. Liberalism is the best system because it enables, encourages, and/or achieves fifteen major values:

- Freedom
- Hard work
- Smart work
- Creative work
- Improving the average standard of living
- Improving the lot of the poor
- Improving the prospects of the outstanding
- More philanthropy
- More social diversity and interestingness
- Happiness
- More religious tolerance
- The decline of sexism and racism
- Peace
- Justice
- The decline of government corruption.

Next, we turn to fifteen powerful arguments against liberalism.

3

Fifteen Arguments against Liberalism

19

Humans are not intelligent enough for freedom. Liberalism is too idealistic. It gives people much freedom and responsibility and expects them to be able to handle it. But most people do not have the knowledge, intelligence, and judgment needed to decide the best course of action for their lives.

We all like to think that we are smart, but the math is cruel. Half of us are below median intelligence, and some of us are considerably lower. So why should we think that freedom is a good policy for everyone?

A free society presupposes that people are *capable* of self-responsible living. That in turn presupposes that they are intelligent enough to do so. And a liberal *democracy* presupposes that the majority will consistently make good political decisions. That also presupposes that they have enough intelligence.

Here is a sobering contrary anecdote. A reader wrote to a columnist with a perplexing math problem he had been debating over dinner with his wife and brother-in-law.[31] Suppose that you pour one cup of 100% bran cereal into a bowl, and then you pour one cup of 40% bran cereal into the same bowl. What percentage of bran is now in the bowl?

The reader's wife said 140%—apparently one should *add* the two percentages to get the right answer. The brother-in-law disagreed, holding that one should *subtract* the lower from the higher percentage, so the correct answer is 60%. The reader himself thought that both answers were wrong—and that the right answer *depends* on whether one first pours the 100% bran or the 40% bran into the bowl.

So we have three individuals who cannot do basic math. Do they have the cognitive skills necessary to make good decisions in our complex, high-tech world? Intellectually, they are nearly helpless to navigate the world—but in the name of freedom the liberals want us to leave them to their own devices.

It gets worse. Perhaps *you* can do basic math. But in a democracy the three citizens above can easily outvote you on any public policy issue. What are the chances that their three math-challenged votes will be better than your one math-informed vote? So liberal democracy is nothing more than the slow suicide of the collectively stupid.[32]

Consequently, a *managed* freedom is best for most people. Some of us are smarter than others. The most intelligent can do social good by making the important decisions for their less intelligent brethren, or at least firmly nudging them in the proper direction.[33] That would be more benevolent than leaving them to their own precarious intelligence.

We should therefore design the political system to assign power to the most intelligent and informed.[34] We should take decision-making power away from the less intelligent—for their own good and the good of society as a whole.

In ancient times, Plato argued that we need philosopher-kings.[35] For our modern science-and-technology-intensive society, we need philosopher-scientist-kings.[36]

The degree of control assigned to government authorities will be tied to the degree of our confidence in people's intellectual capacities. The more pessimistic we are about the average intelligence, the more wide-ranging decision-making powers we will give to the authorities.[37]

But perhaps most people need guidance only on complicated matters. If so, then we can include some democratic elements. We can permit the majority of voters to determine who will have the authority to make important decisions on their behalf. To make voters' choices easier, we can have political parties pre-select suitably intelligent candidates, and voters will then choose the best from among them.

Once elected, though, the political representatives will face a problem. The world is complex and that many important decisions must be made—but they themselves do not always have the necessary knowledge to decide wisely.

So our representatives will create a series of government agencies staffed with intelligent experts—about manufacturing and trade, banking and finance, food and drink, pharmaceuticals and medicine, transportation, and the education of our children. The expert agencies will be empowered to make the necessary decisions. Citizens can then make choices, but within a framework selected and enforced by their society's most intelligent and informed members.

In that system, those of lower intelligence are protected from the consequences of their ignorance in their private lives, and the rest of us are protected from the consequences of their voting in our public lives.

20

Human nature is too immoral for freedom. An ancient myth tells of a man named Gyges who found a magical ring. Gyges was a shepherd, responsible for tending his village's sheep as they grazed in the meadows away in the hills. His job was lonely, poorly paid, and most of the time he smelled like a sheep.

But in a cave one day Gyges found a gold ring with a jewel in it. He put the ring on his finger and discovered something amazing: when he turned the ring so the jewel faced inward, he became invisible. When he turned the jewel outward, he again became visible.

One can predict what happened next: a crime wave. Gyges abandoned the sheep and returned to the village. Expensive things were stolen. Women were raped. People were killed. There were no witnesses. Gyges moved on to greater conquests—stealing, deceiving, and killing his way to the top. He eventually murdered the king, put himself on the throne, and took the dead king's wife to bed as his own queen.

Ancient storytellers from Herodotus to Plato used the Gyges myth to meditate upon political ethics.[38] Gyges, they argued, is not a peculiar individual—he is everyman and a stand-in for *human nature*. The ring is a metaphor for *power*—the power to do what one wants without consequences. And what does Gyges want? He wants what any human being wants—wealth, sex, revenge upon one's enemies, and unendingly more.

The ring's power of invisibility means that he can now satisfy his strongest desires in the easiest ways possible. He need not work hard for money. He need not elaborately woo women. He need not devise complicated plans to kill his enemies.

Thus, in philosophy-mathematics: *Human Nature* plus *Power* equals *Crime*. Humans are beings of predatory passions—greed, lust, anger, and more. But to the extent that we act on our strongest passions we make social living either brutish or impossible.

The ring's power gave Gyges the *freedom* to do anything he wanted. But clearly freedom is socially destructive, because it unleashes human nature and human nature is degenerate. So if we want a peaceful and productive society, then freedom is the enemy.

Gyges is a Greek myth, but we get a similar account of humanity as we move east to other ancient Mediterranean cultures.

In the book of Genesis, a common source for the Western world's three major religions, we learn that Eve and Adam, in their first significant act of freedom, *stole* the fruit.[39] In the next generation, Cain *killed* Abel.[40] Subsequent generations, left free to their own devices, constantly lied, raped, assaulted, massacred, and more—until God returned in the generation of Noah. God saw the corruption that humans had wrought and decided to kill them and start over.[41] But even in the do-over era, human nature again outed itself and caused the same destructive outcomes. Hence the doctrine of Original Sin.

In both religious and secular form, the argument is that human nature is dominated by desires that make us unfit for freedom. Freedom is a kind of power, but power either corrupts us[42] or releases an already-corrupt human nature.[43]

Given this grim truth, what should we do to make social living possible? Return to the philosophy-math: If human nature combined with freedom leads to badness,[44] then to avoid the badness we either have to change human nature or take away freedom. If we cannot change human nature, then we must focus on stifling its negative manifestations.

One way is through *fear*. Before he found the ring, Gyges did not act upon his passions because he was afraid of being caught. The ring eliminated that fear, and his passions were unleashed. So we should ensure that humans remain the way Gyges was before the ring: relatively powerless and afraid of the authorities.

In secular form, we can give the police and the courts great surveillance and punishment powers. Or in religious form, we can make people believe in a God who is always watching and who will punish them strictly. "Fear of the Lord is the beginning of wisdom,"[45] for example. But whether secular or religious, we must instill the fear of authoritarian forces to counter natural human depravity.

Fear of *external* powers like the police or the gods is one check,[46] but we can also use *internal* checks by teaching people to stifle themselves. Instead of *political fear*, use *moral guilt*.[47]

If the problem is *greed*, for example, then from infancy we can teach children a moral lesson: that loving money is the root of all evil.[48] When they naturally come to desire money, an internal battle will be waged between their greed and their taught belief that wanting money is immoral. The guilt will not work perfectly, but it will make them more likely to suppress their greed.

Or if the problem is *lust*, then teach sexual abstinence as the moral ideal.[49] It will not work all of the time, but sexual guilt will help dampen the lust. Or if the problem is *anger*, then teach that one should always forgive.[50] The natural desire for vengeance and the taught morality of forgiveness will fight mightily within them, and if we feel guilty about wanting revenge then they will be less likely to seek it.

In summary: If the myths of Gyges, Eve, and Cain capture a deep truth about human nature, then we have only two solutions: a morality of guilt or a politics of fear—or both. Freedom is power, and human nature will abuse it, so liberalism is a non-starter.

21

Liberalism is amorally self-interested. Liberals often cite the *practical consequences of* free societies—the increasing quantity of goods available, rising life expectancy, and so on—but we must question the *moral motivation* of its agents.

The great moral teachers in history have almost always condemned self-interest. Yet liberalism consistently emphasizes the self: *my* freedom,[51] *my* privacy,[52] *my* pursuit of happiness,[53] *my* right to life.[54] With its individualistic emphasis upon *Me* and *Mine*, liberalism denies the proper moral basis of society.[55]

In the economic sphere, for instance, many liberals argue that free-market capitalism has proved to be more economically productive than socialism has. They draw the conclusion that capitalism is better. But any system that depends upon the profit motive is by definition an *unethical* system[56]—and any system that strives to replace the profit-motive with non-profit motivation is by definition an *ethical* system. Therefore, socialism or feudalism—or any non-profit-based system—is more moral even if it is not as practical.

Further: in the personal sphere, liberals emphasize the pursuit of personal happiness and insist that individuals have the freedom to define their own pleasures and decide how they are going to achieve them. Liberalism therefore subordinates *duty* to self-interested *inclinations*, when the opposite is true.[57] Liberalism denies the deep moral truth that morality is about doing what one is obligated to do. Duty means doing what is right whether one wants to or not and whether it brings one any pleasure or not.[58]

And about life in general, the liberals insist upon each individual's right to life and deny the authority of higher moral entities to insist upon sacrifice when necessary. Yet the willingness to sacrifice oneself selflessly—and the social imperative of sacrifice—are the heart of ethics.[59]

In summary, while liberalism's self-interest may be *productive*, its *What's-in-it-for-me?* egoism undercuts any *moral* worth it may have.[60] Manure might produce a flower, but we hold our noses in its presence.

22

Liberalism's individualism is atomistic. Man is primarily a *social* being, not an *individual* one. As a result, liberalism undermines one's humanity by denying one's deepest social needs and social identity.

In the modern world especially, liberalism has stressed *individualism*, and as a consequence it has lessened the individual's identification with family,[61] community,[62] nation,[63] race,[64] and even God.[65] It has stressed *independence* and so encouraged individuals to see dependence as a weakness to be denied. And it has stressed *freedom* and so urged individuals to seek themselves outside of or even in rebellion against the social.

The result is individuals who are alone, isolated, and at their core, empty of true humanity. The rugged individualist who rides off alone into the sunset. The financier who isolates himself with his millions from the rest of society's struggles. The shock artist who feels the need to spit in the face of decent society in order to find her artistic uniqueness. The city-dweller who—even though living among millions—feels alienated. All are products of liberalism's false theory of human individual identity.[66]

The truth is that humans are made by their societies. They are born into social units—families, neighborhoods, and larger social and political units—that define their roles.[67] They are born into a language that shapes their thinking and gives them a social-linguistic group identity.[68] They are born malleable in their tastes and values, which are formed by prevailing social practices and norms. And their highest aspirations are realized in achieving their social being.[69] The individual is a myth, and attempts to isolate the individual lead only to pathologies.

Consequently, the best society for human beings will be one that puts the social above the individual,[70] that encourages each of us to put the group's needs before our own,[71] and that when necessary demands that the individual be subordinated to society's higher standing.[72]

The atomistic individualism that liberalism leads to is bad not only for individuals, as it undercuts their true identity as social beings,[73] but also for society itself, which is the only vehicle through which the highest human values can be realized.[74]

23

Liberalism is materialistic. Liberalism may generate material wealth, but its emphasis upon such prosperity fosters materialistic values that are trivial, ultimately empty, and even undercut our capacity for pursuing truly important values.[75]

Advocates of free markets typically emphasize material measures of success. For example, they measure production and consumption activity—gross domestic product, how financial markets are performing, the number of automobiles purchased, and the size of people's homes. That is, they measure value by means of money and physical quantities, with the assumption that more is better.

This sends a wrong signal to consumers. It leads them to define their worth in terms of their possessions and so to believe that they need unendingly more.[76]

That in turn leads to many social pathologies. The basest material desires—for food and sex—are often the easiest to satisfy. So driven by consumer demand, the free market devotes disproportionate amounts of resources to those materialist values. Another is that human social-psychology of the "keeping up with the Joneses" variety causes unhealthy competition: my neighbor has acquired some material good, so I feel compelled to acquire it myself so as not to be perceived as less worthy. Yet another pathology is a cultural version of Gresham's Law: free-market capitalism is driven largely by the mass market, but mass taste and culture are at best low-to-moderate, so the market for lower-quality material goods tends to drive out quality cultural goods.[77]

A further pathology is that a free-market society increasingly develops sophisticated and powerful institutions devoted to selling and consumerism. That is to say, its advertising industry makes the problem worse.[78]

Advertisers use sophisticated psychology and expend large amounts of society's resources, often in the service of selling trivialities. Millions are spent to promote a new style of sneakers or hair gel while budgets are cut for education and the fine arts. Often we do not even "know" that we need something until advertising induces us to feel that we "need" it.[79]

Therefore we must reject liberalism's insistence upon unlimited freedom in production and consumption choice, and we must reject its insistence upon unbridled freedom of advertising. Good social policy should guide producers and consumers away from base materialism and ensure that advertising directs people toward genuinely valuable goods.[80]

In stronger form, our argument is that the empty materialism of liberal capitalism causes a value crisis for mankind.[81] We are not merely animals but creatures with strong *psychological* and *spiritual* needs.[82] But capitalism's materialism—while it generates lots of stuff—empties our lives of genuine meaning, leaving us vulnerable to neurosis and nihilism.[83]

If we ask what a life of genuine meaning is, then of course a variety of philosophical possibilities will emerge. But the main thrust of our argument is that the government must take an active hand in human psychological and spiritual development. Just as we cannot leave provision of healthy material needs to the free market, we cannot expect the free market to fulfill humans' true psychological and spiritual needs.[84] "Statecraft," to borrow a line, "is soulcraft."[85]

In moderate form, a non-materialist society will use its government to find a healthy *balance* between our physical and our psychological wants, between our material and our spiritual needs. Government policy will be directed toward curbing the materialist excesses of liberal capitalism and toward supplying remedies for its psychological and spiritual deficits.[86]

In strongest form, anti-materialism will require government policy to *deny* the significance of physical values at all and to direct humanity in a purely spiritual direction. Materialists make physical life on Earth the highest—note their obsession with increasing life expectancy, as if human beings are merely bodies to be preserved indefinitely. But while life on Earth is short, life after physical death is forever. Our true vocation is to live and die so as to be worthy of ultimate justice.[87]

So if liberalism leads to materialism and materialism is anti-spiritual, then liberalism must be rejected at its root.

The fundamental three sources of immorality are the desires for wealth, sex, and doing one's own will.[88] Note that the great moral teachers in both the major Eastern[89] and Western religious traditions have always made the anti-materialist, ascetic virtues the first step toward ethical idealism: *poverty*,[90] *chastity*,[91] and *obedience*.

Note especially that the first *sin* in the Garden of Eden was *disobedience*. Consequently, the first *virtue* is *obedience*, not liberty. A moral society will be one in which material pursuits are minimized as much as possible, and one in which its members are willing to sacrifice their physical possessions, their physical satisfactions,[92] and even their physical lives[93] in order to achieve spiritual fulfillment.

24

Liberal societies are boring. We do not need to glamorize tribal or feudal life in order to see that modern liberalism's replacement is another form of tedium occasionally sprinkled with low-grade pleasures.

The imperative of liberal capitalism is: *productiveness*. So it has proceeded to transform the workplace. Agriculture was mechanized. Factories filled with machines and workers as their semi-robotic adjuncts. Corporations populated their office towers with cubicle farms filled with business-suits.[94]

Everything was more productive—but at a cost: *mass* production, sameness, standardization. Even time was made uniform and work became shift-work—whether 9-to-5 or the graveyard shift—with a demand that all workers, whether blue- or white-collar, conform to the pace.[95]

The same stultification of liberal capitalism carries over when we turn from production to consumption.

The modern world gave mankind freedom, just as liberalism claims. It did lower the barriers of inequality and improve their material condition. But look at what its free people chose: the *soft* life of suburban sprawl and shopping malls and *lowest-common-denominator* entertainment. They chose to be *conformist* in their tastes and fashions and to avoid causing friction with their neighbors and in-laws. They traded their souls for *comforts* and quiet, low-grade hedonism. They chose *safety* and the *risk-avoiding* life. And they call it "progress."[96]

We can label this set of values: the *bourgeois* code. The bourgeoisie's top values are security, standardization, conformity, and peace.[97]

But man does not live by bread, Internet porn and cat pictures alone. He needs a quest, a mission, a sense of his life as a grand adventure.[98] Yet modern liberalism has created and enshrined a petty and *inauthentic* life.

So a human being in quest of an authentic life must *break with* liberalism's stultifying bourgeois lifestyle.[99] It must reject the soft imperialism of liberalism's standardized culture and its passive-aggressive demands that everyone be *nice*.

Authenticity will embrace uniqueness, risk-taking, danger—and the exalting experience of everything being at stake, even one's own precious life.

The quest for authenticity can take several forms. One is via *Religion*—a religion that is born of disgust with the complacency of the apathetic herd and its soul-deadening pursuits. By rejecting everyday society and the ordinary pursuits of bourgeois life, one can free one's spirit, one's soul, and one's true self and become open to enthusiasm, ecstasy, or nirvana.[100]

Another route is via *Art*. The low-grade art of the bourgeoisie is of course beneath contempt—it is about copying tired old tropes,[101] it is about prettiness and easy beauty,[102] it is kitsch.[103] Consequently, the journey of one's artistic development may require shocking the bourgeoisie to demonstrate to them, contemptuously, and oneself that one has truly broken with them. But once so freed, one can genuinely seek the original and the sublime.[104]

Yet another authentic possibility is *War*. Liberals of course want peace so that their money-making trade networks are not disturbed. But the point of life is not crass money-making. And the commercial life is not suited for the highest human development, as it cultivates the softer and, shall we say, more effeminate, shopkeeper traits: it wants orderly ledgers, the comforts of home and ordinary life,[105] and to be distracted from its petty troubles and entertained.[106] By contrast, war at its best inculcates more vigorous and hardy traits that lift humans to their true potential, individually and communally, as it seeks the great deed and the deadly serious mission.[107]

For any of us to live fully, humankind needs predators more than traders,[108] self-sacrificers more than self-seekers,[109] and those who embrace pain and difficulty more than those who want pleasure and ease.[110]

25

Power is the reality, so liberalism is naïve. Liberalism makes freedom the top social value, but that is naïve because freedom is neither an accurate description of human social reality nor the most desirable value.

Life is about power. Weeds and grasses vie for soil and sunlight. The insect eats the grass. The rat eats the insect. The hawk catches the rat and devours it. The man captures the hawk and puts it in a cage—and makes it fly according to *his* will.

Power relations dominate reality. *Within* any power framework, there can be sub-areas of peace, freedom, and affection. The alpha lion may let the other lions eat after he has had his fill, and he may play occasionally with the cubs. But those are interludes with an ongoing power struggle—the younger beta lions are waiting for their chance to dethrone him, neighboring prides are probing for weakness, the pride will soon need to kill again, and battles against diseases and the elements are constant.

Human life is continuous with the rest of organic life, and all of human history is testament to this fact.[111] Life is struggle—a conflict between life and death and a choice between dominance and submission. War is not merely an extension of politics but our basic metaphysical condition.[112]

The relations between men and women,[113] competing businesses,[114] and even the pursuit of knowledge[115]—with its claimed imperatives of objectivity and intellectual freedom—are manifestations of exploitative power.

So we must reject liberalism's insistence upon the moral rights of individuals to their own freedom.[116] That philosophy may be a rhetorical strategy used by the weaker to get what they want[117]—namely, a zone of safety free from the stronger—but the powerful have no need for such devices and will always find a way to wrest what they desire from whatever system happens to be in place. And they will do it as a matter of right[118]—as long as we understand *right* to be a clear-eyed acceptance of realism.[119]

The reality and the glory of life is the acquisition and exercise of power over others. As the cliché has it, all really is fair in love and war. When we define normative concepts such as *justice*, we might strive to mask the underlying power relations. But the battle over definitions is simply one more dimension in the struggle for dominance, and definitions that delude our enemies give us an advantage over them. And of course when we are strong enough we will dispense with the masks and proclaim straightforwardly that justice is whatever the powerful want it to be.[120]

Domination is therefore basic to the political.[121] Those who acquire dominion power will be those who recognize this reality of the human condition and who do not flinch from using the stratagems necessary to maintain it.[122] Any other philosophy of life is a foolish and childish attempt to escape from the harsh adult realities of life and death.

26

Liberalism does not guarantee that everyone's basic needs will be met. Liberalism attempts to guarantee freedom but it does not guarantee that everyone's basic needs will be met.[123] Yet on the most fundamental requirements of life, we should not cold-heartedly force anyone to trade-off between liberty's risks and being secure in one's basic needs. Security is more important than liberty.

Especially in the wealthy parts of the world, there is no excuse for allowing poverty. Yet in such places, the rich typically indulge themselves in luxuries and frivolities.[124] But survival needs are of greater moral significance than luxuries, and morality requires that we sacrifice the inessential to the essential. So it is a matter of moral obligation that those with more than they need provide for those with less than they need.[125]

Most people in comfortable material circumstances, however, seem unwilling voluntarily to act to meet the greater needs of others.[126] Consequently, when voluntary sacrifice is not forthcoming in sufficient quantities, some measure of government redistribution is warranted.

Further: human *dignity* is a basic right,[127] but there is no dignity in poverty and there is no dignity in having to ask for charity. So—as an institution morally responsible for protecting human rights—the government should grant to each human being by right at least the minimum necessary to avoid poverty.

A standard liberal response is to cite capitalism's productivity and to argue that the poorer parts of the world can become richer by adopting free markets and property rights. But that is to focus on the long term—perhaps the very long term. In the short-term, people are suffering and dying.

Another standard liberal response is to cite everyone's self-responsibility and to assert their competence at satisfying their basic needs. But this overlooks the vulnerable status of children, especially in poorer nations. If *adults* in such circumstances struggle and often fail to provide for their own needs, it is too much to expect their *children* to succeed in doing so. And without their basic needs being met during their crucial developmental stages, children will not grow into adults with a fighting chance at life. Our social responsibility therefore extends at a minimum to providing basic sustenance to the young.[128]

We can argue about what range of services should be considered basic needs—food and drink, education, healthcare, infrastructure, safety, sex—but in contrast to the vagaries of free markets only governments have the power and the will to ensure that basic needs are met consistently.[129]

Global capitalism, by contrast, has led to a world in which millions are not provided for. A moral social system will recognize the interdependence of all of humanity[130] and address itself to redressing the under-supply of basic goods to many.[131]

27

Liberalism is unfair. Fairness is a basic moral concept.[132] Fairness is often connected to *desert*—ensuring that people get what they deserve. And to ensure as much as possible that people do get what they deserve, a fair society will design society's rules and institutions with that purpose in mind.

But liberalism is fundamentally unfair in two important ways: many people start out with undeserved advantages in life, and liberalism's rules both perpetuate the unfairness and enable many to acquire further outsized and undeserved social rewards.

No one deserves his or her starting place in life. In the great lottery of human existence, some are born with greater natural endowments than others and some are born into favorable social circumstances. Individuals are born more or less healthy and with more or less potential for intelligence, endurance, and bodily strength. Individuals are born into more or less wealthy families, neighborhoods, and societies and with more or less opportunities for education and character development. Consequently, the decisive factors for each of us are a matter of luck[133]—they are not within our control and so we cannot claim any form of moral credit for them.

But a liberal society simply takes this undeserved initial distribution of social goods as its unquestioned starting point. It then leaves people free to find their own way and considers as fair whatever results follow from free exchanges. Yet if the initial conditions of a society were a matter of undeserved luck, then the resulting distribution of goods is also undeserved.

Since gaining from undeserved advantages is unfair, a society concerned with fairness will make efforts to redress the undeserved advantages.[134] This will require either direct redistribution from the advantaged to the disadvantaged or an indirect redistribution by designing rules and institutions to the advantage of the initially disadvantaged.

A further form of unfairness stems from liberalism's claim about the individual nature of wealth creation. It emphasizes the self-made man and gives outsized recognition and monetary rewards to such. The architect takes the credit for the building, ignoring the hundreds or thousands of workers who actually built the structure. The industrialist puts his name on the factory and takes the largest share of the profits, overlooking the fact that the factory's output is the result of collective effort.[135] The banker and the venture capitalist collect interest and take profits, when the wealth was actually created by the efforts of others.[136] And every one of us is dependent upon the achievements of the many others who went before us.

Our initial life circumstance was made possible by our parents and their parents before them. Our upbringing is also due to our parents and others,[137] including the government's rules about marriage, family, and the requirements of children's nurturance and education.[138]

Consequently, we all owe a debt to the broader society to which we belong. Debt brings with it them an obligation to repay. Yet liberal capitalism urges us see ourselves as the authors of our own lives and to take more for ourselves from society rather than recognizing our indebtedness.[139]

28

Equality is threatened by freedom. Liberalism does allow for many important equalities. It agrees that we should judge everyone by the same general standards, that adults should be equally free to participate in the political process, and that there should be equality before the law.

But liberalism does *not* allow for economic and more radical forms of social equality, and its making freedom more fundamental than equality only guarantees that inequalities will result. Radical equality across *all* social dimensions should be a fundamental imperative.[140]

Economic inequality is both morally objectionable in itself and leads to pathological social consequences. In the beginning, we should recognize that the resources of the Earth belong to all human beings equally. So those who take from the common stock and assert a private property right are taking from the rest of us.[141]

Liberals sometimes respond that allowing private property unleashes the productive power of the profit motive and the free market, which in turn benefits everyone, including the least advantaged. So, they assert, some departures from strict equality are justified.[142]

But once initiated, such departures from equality will be difficult to contain and will lead only to further and worse inequalities.

It is the natural tendency of free markets towards concentrations of wealth and monopolies. Free-market capitalism is a system of *competitive between unequals*—rather than a system of *cooperation with equals*—and successive rounds of capitalist competition lead to winners and losers. The economic winners are then able to establish powerful concentrations in major industries and to dominate their markets. Aside from the threats to consumer this poses—monopoly pricing, for example—such big businesses can make it difficult-to-impossible for new and smaller businesses to gain entry into the market and compete successfully.[143]

Inequalities of wealth exacerbate other social inequalities. The richer are better able to influence and use their wealth even to corrupt the political process. The elite tend to socialize, marry, and inter-breed among themselves, thus perpetuating their high social status. Unequally wealthy neighborhoods contribute to social stratification, as a given school district may spend a small amount of money per year per student for education while a neighboring district spends many times that amount.

As a result, even if the poorer members of society are raised above subsistence and absolute poverty, their *relative* poverty will cause social frictions.[144] The poorer will envy the richer and the richer will lord it over the poorer.[145]

Therefore, even if liberalism does produce greater overall prosperity—

that is not worth the trade-off damage that it does to equality. It is better that society be less rich and more equal.[146]

We should, accordingly, make every effort now to redistribute goods, opportunities, and statuses equally. The rich themselves should feel an obligation to make society more equal, both for moral and prudential reasons.[147] But the rich's voluntary efforts are unlikely to be sufficient, so active government redistribution is necessary.

Liberals sometimes point out that even if we make people again equal, inequalities will simply re-assert themselves. Differences in natural endowments, efforts, and luck will again lead to economic inequalities.[148] But this means only that ongoing government management is needed to maintain equality as much as is possible. Also, with proper education and social conditioning,[149] we can perhaps alter those differences in human nature that cause social inequality.[150]

But achieving equality will likely be impossible in a global economy where nations and regions have different economic strengths. Liberals like to point out that the principle of comparative advantage combined with international free markets leads nations to specialize in production and to then trade with each other to mutual advantage. But it is impossible to imagine how such an arrangement will not lead to some nations becoming richer than others and the inhabitants of each nation desiring, often enviously, the superior advantages of other nations. That can only exacerbate international tensions and contribute to the threat of war.

So to avoid all of these dangers, we face a choice between two broad options: one is to work toward a human society united under a single government charged with maintaining global equality—and the other is to move toward a number of small-scale, simpler, localized societies that keep their separateness in order to maintain the internal equality of their membership.[151]

While economic matters are important, we should attend also to other dimensions of social equality.

In more radical and general forms of egalitarian thinking, privileging oneself in *any* way is counter to the moral imperative of equality. To say *I prefer myself to others* or *I prefer some people to others* is to apply a standard that allows inequality. Countering inequality generally has implications for relations between the races, ethnicities, sexes, the family, and humanity in general.

Unfortunately, most people tend to identify themselves with their own racial and ethnic groups.[152] Left unchecked and in combination with liberalism, such identifications can lead to racist and ethnocentric groupthink, and such groupthink in turn combined with a belief in property rights is complicit in race-based slavery.[153]

Further, liberalism in combination with biological differences between males and females can lead to unequal outcomes for men and women. Gender equality therefore requires active intervention to achieve both more equal opportunities and outcomes.[154]

Family members tend to love and privilege their own—husbands and wives, parents and children, brothers and sisters. That in practice means that they treat unequally their neighbors, fellow citizens, and the rest of humanity.[155]

Therefore, a full commitment to equality as our fundamental moral goal requires a rejection of liberalism's leaving people free to evaluate and interact with others by almost any standards they choose. The thrust of liberalism puts it in tension with equality in all areas of social life. So allowable freedoms must be nested within a broader social mandate of achieving full equality.[156]

29

Scarcity means that freedom is dog-eat-dog. We live in a world of scarce resources. *Scarcity* is the condition in which the demand for a good outstrips its supply by a significant amount.

The world has only so many resources—mineral, land-based, and atmospheric. At any given time, quantities are finite, and in the future there is a necessary finite limit to possible growth.[157] At the same time, there is increasingly more desire to consume those resources. The human population has increased dramatically, which means that collectively we are putting greater demands on the Earth. Not only that, as we have become more prosperous we are no longer content with simplicity but require more resources to maintain our complicated lifestyles—we eat more and more varied foods, we live in larger homes, we travel further, and more.

In sum: *resources are limited, while human wants are unlimited*. Consequently, scarcity means that not everyone's wants can be met. How then should we decide whose wants will be satisfied and whose will not?

In nature, the balance between the supply of resources and any animal population's demand for them is maintained by conflict, disease, and starvation. Animals compete for food resources and for mates, in the case of those that reproduce sexually. While available food resources can go up and down in the short term, they remain relatively constant over time. Meanwhile, animal populations tend to increase geometrically.[158] Eventually the population's demand outstrips the available food resources, and especially when that point is reached the animals fight, often brutally.[159] Those that are weaker tend to lose the battles; the die immediately or go hungry and eventually succumb to the elements. Those that are stronger tend to win the battles; they eat and survive to have sex and reproduce themselves, thus passing their traits on to the next generation.[160] And the battles carry on unendingly across the generations.

If we believe that humans are a part of nature, then we are driven to apply the logic of the same brutal dynamics to human society.[161] So we ask again, *How should we decide whose wants will be satisfied and whose will not?*

Liberalism says that we should do so by means of competition and property rights. But of course in the capitalistic competition for scarce resources there will necessarily be winners and losers. The *stronger*—that is, the quicker, the more physically powerful, the more cunning—will prevail against the *weaker*—the slower, the less muscular, and the less ruthless. And as we come to recognize that we are all locked in a zero-sum struggle,[162] the competition will intensify and will bring out the worst in us.[163]

But since liberalism simply leaves us free and urges us to act as we wish, it is encouraging us to act as predators—or allowing us to be victimized by predators.[164] This survival-of-the-fittest mentality[165] means that liberal capitalism is a species of Social Darwinism.[166]

The scarcity-driven *economic* conflict naturally spills over into *political* conflict. When government's leaders face or fear a scarcity of resources that are essential to their nation's interests, international political tensions will increase and war will become more likely.[167]

As a species, we *must* keep our human demand for resources in balance with supply. To do so we have only two options: either the law-of-the-jungle method of free-market capitalism—which will only further diminish the supply and increase the demand—or the calmer and more humane method of government management. With some significant degree of intervention or perhaps full socialism, we can replace competition for resources with cooperation in managing them,[168] and instead of letting people breed willy-nilly we can formulate a rational population policy that keeps supply and demand in balance.[169]

30

Liberalism is unsustainable. Many parts of the world are environmental hells. They are dirty and depleted, making them unhealthy and economically unsustainable. Human greed is the culprit: self-interest manifested in the profit motive and institutionalized by capitalism. *Self-*

interest means that people want more at the least cost to themselves. *Profit now* means using up resources sooner rather than later and getting rid of the waste the easiest way possible. And *capitalism*'s rule-minimalism only serves to encourage wanton behavior.[170]

Liberalism's unsustainability occurs on both the production and the consumption sides of the economic equation. Its imperative of greater production causes resources to be depleted at an unsustainable rate, and its emphasis upon greater consumption causes unsustainable amounts of waste.

On the production side of the equation, a classic example is that of herdsmen using a common pasture.[171] Each herdsman is a self-interested farmer who wants to put as many cows as he can into the pasture because each additional cow increases his profits. But each additional cow means that less pasture is available for the other herdsmen's cows. The other profit-seeking herdsmen are of course doing the same thing, and as more cows are added the pasture's grasses become depleted more quickly. The herdsmen become locked into a zero-sum competition that leads to the destruction of the pasture.

We can generalize from the pasture to all resources. Resources are limited, but the dynamic of profit and competition necessarily leads to a violation of those limits.[172]

The solution is clear: If short-sighted self-interest is the problem—if anti-social profit seeking is the problem—and if the capitalist free market's anything-goes *laissez-faire* is the problem—then the fix will require an institution able to override selfish profit-seeking and impose rules about resource use that take into account society as a whole's long-term needs. That is to say, the government should manage society's resources.

In the case of the herdsmen, the government should decide how many cows each may put out and for how long. It should mandate that each herdsman does his fair share of maintenance and improvements in the pasture—weeding, fence-building, well-digging, waste collection. It will hire police to ensure that none of the herdsmen cheat or shirk. And it will impose taxes in order to fund the rule-making and monitoring. That is to say, good environmental policy will require some combination of rationing, conscription, policing, and taxation.

Turning to the consumption side of the economic equation: at the end of the consumer process is a waste product—packaging to be thrown away and items that break or otherwise reach the end of their useful life. The production process itself generates significant amounts of waste—solid garbage, liquids, and gases that end up in our landfills, waterways, and atmosphere. But liberal capitalism's celebration of consumerism means that increasingly more waste will be generated, and its self-interested motivation means that the waste will be disposed of in the lowest-cost manner possible and in ways that shift the costs and risks to others.

Consequently, government regulation is also essential to reduce the quantity of waste produced, by some combination of controls on packaging, mandating recycling, or reducing the human population.[173]

A sustainable resource policy requires some measure of authoritarianism. At a minimum, it implies increasing the powers of existing government agencies to regulate resource use and waste disposal; at a maximum, it implies a revolution against capitalism[174] and the need for a world government.[175]

31

Liberalism is socially inefficient. A liberal system leads to lack of coordination at the social level. Liberalism decentralizes decision-making and action to the individual level, and that leads to much inefficiency, counter-productive conflict, and social weakness.

Within their own spheres, individuals may very well be able to judge what needs to be done. But coordination as the social level does not happen automatically or by free-market magic. Society-wide efficiency requires a broader cognitive perspective and the power to coordinate scattered social resources.[176]

Just as any boat with many oars needs a coxswain, every team needs a coach, and every army needs a general—every society needs leadership that establishes goals, determines strategy, and motivates and directs the subordinate units.

Consider a factory in which each worker is capable of doing his or her own job competently. Nonetheless, a foreman is needed to coordinate the efforts of the workers in his team. The foreman's broader perspective enables him to see what adjustments are necessary and so to direct the individual workers appropriately. As we scale up to the level of the factory as a whole, the general manager's perspective enables her to see what the various foremen in different parts of the factory cannot see—the connections between activities in receiving, manufacturing, inventory, sales, finance, and more—and so to direct the foremen to make adjustments as necessary. The same principles hold as we consider the industry sector that the particular factory is operating in, as well as when we consider each industry sector as part of an economy as a whole. At each level, coordinating management is needed.[177]

Otherwise the tendency is to activity that is at best disconnected and at worst counter-productive. Only proper leadership can integrate information available only at the macro level and formulate long-term plans.[178]

What holds for the domestic economy also holds for foreign policy and national security. The problem is not only that individuals have narrow *value-interests* that lead them to discount society-as-a-whole's military needs—the shopkeeper who wants only to stay home and conduct business, the mother who does not want to expose her son to risk, everyone's petty rivalries that lead them to fight each other rather than pulling together against a common enemy. The problem is *cognitive*: most citizens have a narrow cognitive focus and are not aware of the demands of the international context.

Liberal societies, history has shown, are therefore vulnerable to centralized cultures. Athenian democratic dithering and the narrowness of its citizen's private commercial interests explain much of why it lost to Sparta, why it was later controlled by Macedon, and why the whole of Greece was taken over by Rome.[179]

Consequently, in all major social sectors—economic, educational, military, and the rest—top-down power is regularly needed to supplement or override bottom-up initiatives, and some form of society-as-a-whole leadership must in principle take precedence over liberalism's decentralization.

32

Liberalism is merely another subjective narrative. Liberals claim that their political philosophy is based upon compelling empirical and theoretical argument. They also claim that liberalism should be applied to all human beings. That is, they present their case as if objectivity and universality were possible to achieve.

Liberalism requires much confidence in the power of reason. It leaves common citizens free to make their own major life choices about friendships, marriage, and religion. It leaves them alone to make their own transactions in a free market, and it urges them to participate politically in a democratic republic. The assumption is that in all of those areas of life individuals are capable of assessing their circumstances objectively and so on balance making good decisions.

Liberalism also requires much confidence in the more sophisticated reason of its theorists. It presupposes that they can assess the historical and contemporary evidence accurately, that it can use the tools of mathematics and the scientific method more generally, and that it can logically integrate all of that into an objective theory that is universally true and good.

The "truth," though, is that objectivity and universality are myths. All claims to evidence, logic, and rational argument are shot through with subjectivity and relativity.

For centuries, many of our strongest religious thinkers have argued that reason is incompetent. Reason, they concluded, fails to prove the existence of God and even purports to show that religion is inconsistent or worse. Reliance upon reason thus leads people away from God.[180] But if people turn away from God, the weakness of their own reason will lead them to nihilism. Liberalism depends upon reason, but reason leads to subjectivism, which leads to relativism, which leads to nihilism.

So, they concluded, to avoid nihilism, we must commit to a strong *faith* in higher authority. Human beings need the submission and obedience of faith, not hubristic independence and confidence in the power of reason. But that defense of faith in God first requires an offensive against reason.[181]

Yet such faith involves a subjective leap, and many intellectuals are unable to make themselves commit to it. Even so, many will continue to advocate religion publically for political reasons. While they personally do not need to believe, they judge that most people cannot get through life without some sort of religion. Religion is the common man or woman's philosophy, giving them personal structure and a reason to follow society's rules. On prudential grounds, therefore, a society's intellectual leaders should encourage widespread belief in the gods or a God. Even if a religion is not true, it is better for society that most people believe that it is true.[182]

Of course, apologists for faith and "noble lie" theorists are merely expressing their subjective preferences for a certain kind of society.

Even so, but a wide variety of considerations support the belief in deep subjectivity.

One is the distinction between *fact* and *value*, *is* and *ought*, *descriptive* and *normative*, a commonplace in modern philosophy. From any set of *factual* statements no *value* statements follow. Purportedly objective truths about how the world *is* do not imply any conclusions about how the world *ought* to be.[183] Values are only subjective preferences.[184] Even propositions of logic and mathematics are empty and merely reflect subjective choices.[185] As a result, no amount of objective data, hard mathematics, and logical argument about liberalism can support the view that liberalism is good or desirable.

Further, human beings' perceptual capacities are subject to occasional illusions and regular relativities—what is sweet to you is bland to me, and what is appealing to eat when one is healthy is repulsive when one is sick.[186] So there is never any guarantee that even our basic observational data are objective or even mutually consistent.

Further still, all interpretations of the data are shaped by prior theoretical commitments. Anyone's theory about the world or a part of it has built into its assumptions about what is real and what is not, what is possible and what is not, what to look for and what to ignore. Necessarily, therefore, our ideological priors infect our interpretations with bias. Even our basic perceptions of the world are laden with theory and so subjective.[187]

Further yet still, human beings are *emotional* as well as rational. We often see and hear only what we want to hear, and the deepest sources of our wants are often unknown to us. Consequently, our beliefs and our value decisions are largely passion-driven rather than the result of reason.[188]

And further yet still, human beings are *social* beings, and they acquire beliefs and values and the very language they think in from their society. What is "rational" is socially conditioned, and since societies vary widely, what is rational is also socially relative.[189]

The point is that *any* theory that bills itself as objective and true is a non-starter,[190] and any political theory that requires a general rationality of its members is naïve.

Instead, we face only a variety of arbitrary subjective options.[191]

Liberals will sometimes grant that everything is subjective and relative—but argue that in order to make social living possible we should all agree to disagree when necessary. That is to say, we should accept *toleration* as our governing principle. We cannot expect or demand that everyone agrees on *substantive* values, but we can push for a universal *procedural* principle: *Live, and let live*. That is admittedly to make an exception by insisting that we treat one principle as generally and objectively true. But in the interest of social peace, the principle of tolerance is the minimally necessary and achievable social objective.

Or if we are of a *Pragmatic* disposition, we will reject robust liberalism as being too absolutist about its principles. Instead, the best we can do is make case-by-case judgments about what works rather than expecting universal principles to apply in all cases. Even toleration may work some circumstances but not in others. We need *flexibility* rather than mechanical rules, and we need to understand that individuals, societies, and the world at large *evolve* over time. What works therefore itself evolves, and we should not be bound by allegedly timeless principles. Admittedly, "what works" is a subjective and relative criterion, but that is our human condition.

Or if we are a *Conservative* of a religious temperament, we will agree that the failures of reason make critical our need for *faith* in a set of absolute, timeless principles. Some beliefs and actions cannot be tolerated socially. And giving ourselves and our political leaders license to do whatever whoever thinks "works" is to abandon society to a free-for-all of depravity and decay. Faith does admittedly require a subjective leap, but perhaps it is our only escape from nihilism.

Or we can, as *Postmoderns* do, feel that the above choices and others are conditioned by our racial, gender, class, and ethnic origins.

Advocates of liberal capitalism in particular are very often white, male, prosperous, and of European background. So their liberalism is merely an expression of *their* socially-subjective conditioning. But if we are of some *other* culture or subculture, then we are under no universalist imperative to suppress or give up the values that shape our social identities and replace them with liberal ones. Such social subjectivism does admittedly lead to a harsher and unending conflicts of cultures, but at least we are not pretending that objective universality is possible.

At most, therefore, liberalism is merely one more subjective option to be considered in the mix of possible systems, and anyone's choice among the possibilities is itself a subjective preference.

33

Freedom does not exist. The core assumption of liberalism is that human beings are by nature free. That is, they have the capacity to make genuine *choices* in their thoughts and actions. That is the basis of treating humans as *moral* agents who are responsible for their behaviors, both positive and negative. And that in turn is the basis for the liberalism's *political* claim that we should respect every human's freedom.

But the fact is that there is *no* freedom, either politically or metaphysically.

In religious form, the argument is the omnipotence of God makes impossible human free will. Free will is supposed to be a species of power, if humans have *some* power, then God cannot have it *all*. Asserting human free will therefore contradicts the infinity of God. The omnipotence of God therefore implies a rigorous predestination: all of reality has been pre-ordained, and God's omniscience implies that he knows all—past, present, and future.[192]

In naturalistic form, the argument is that all of reality is governed by a cause-and-effect matrix that leaves no room for volition. The iron laws of physics, chemistry, biology and the other sciences describe the natural world in deterministic terms. Human beings are physical-chemical-biological complexes embedded within broader systems of physical-chemical-biological complexes. All of us are subject to gravity and to chemical and biological processes—and in the mathematics that describes it all, two plus two always equals four. Cause and effect does not somehow stop with humans. Everything we do is an effect of a set of prior causal factors, which are themselves effects of prior causes, and so on forever into the past. Everything we do in turn becomes part of the set of causal factors that determine subsequent effects, and so on forever into the future.[193]

We can of course continue to debate whether the determining causes are primarily theological,[194] biological,[195] environmental,[196] or some weighted combination of them.

But the point is that the feeling of volition is an *illusion*—an epiphenomenal byproduct of underlying causal forces.[197] There is no free will, and consequently no choice, and consequently no responsibility, and consequently no morality, and consequently no point to liberalism.

So we should get rid of all normative language—or recognize that our use of normative language is merely one more causally-deterministic outcome. Some people are determined to say *Liberalism is good!* and others are determined to say *Liberalism is bad!* Some people are made to act "liberally" and others are made to act "illiberally." In any case, no ultimate evaluative significance can be attached to anyone's expressions or actions, and it is pointless to argue about liberalism.[198]

34

Summary and Transition. Liberalism should be rejected because it undermines, fails to achieve, or contradicts fifteen major truths or values. Liberalism:

- Over-estimates average intelligence
- Underestimates human depravity
- Is based on amoral self-interest
- Is atomistic
- Is materialistic
- Is boring
- Denies the priority of power
- Does not guarantee basic needs
- Is unfair
- Undermines equality
- Is dog-eat-dog
- Is unsustainable
- Is inefficient
- Is merely a subjective narrative
- Is epiphenomenal.

Next, we turn to comparing the thirty arguments for and against liberalism.

4

Conclusion—Arguments in Collision

35

One's next project is to compare and evaluate the arguments. Which are true? Or at least strongest? The purpose of a primer is not to argue a position but to put the reader in an informed position to make the judgments about which position is best. Each argument can be evaluated on its own merits, but it can also be useful to weigh directly opposed arguments against each other. If for example, one side argues that increasing material prosperity is good while the other says materialism is bad, then one realizes that one needs to make an ethical judgment about material value. Or if one side says that respecting free choice is a fundamental while the other says free choice is an illusion, then one knows one must make a metaphysical judgment about free will. Or if one side claims that facts and logic supports its conclusions while the other says that value conclusions are only subjective narratives, then it is clear that one needs to make some decisions about epistemology.

So to aid with that judgment project here are two tables juxtaposing the claims of the fifteen arguments for liberalism and the fifteen against.

Liberalism: Pro and Con

First, the claims simply in the order presented below.

For liberalism	Against liberalism:
Respects freedom	Over-estimates average intelligence
Incentivizes hard work	Underestimates human depravity
Smarter work	Is based on amoral self-interest
More creative work	Is atomistic
Improves the average standard of living	Is materialistic
Improves the lot of the poor	Is boring
Improves the prospects of the outstanding	Denies the priority of power
More philanthropy	Does not guarantee basic needs
More social diversity and interest-ingness	Is unfair
Increases happiness	Undermines equality
More religious tolerance	Is dog-eat-dog
Decreases sexism and racism	Is unsustainable
Incentivizes peace	Is inefficient
Is more just	Is merely a subjective narrative
Lessens government corruption	Is epiphenomenal

Second, a chart with the claims reorganized to juxtapose those that are arguing about similar types of issue.

Type of issue	For liberalism	Against liberalism:
Metaphysics	Respects freedom	Is epiphenomenal Denies the priority of power
Epistemology	Smart work Creative work Hard work	Over-estimates average intelligence Is inefficient
Aesthetics	More social diversity and interestingness	Is boring
Ethics Metaphysics	Improves average standard of living Improves prospects of the outstanding	Is unsustainable Is materialistic
Ethics	Improves the lot of the poor Increases philanthropy	Does not guarantee basic needs Undermines equality
Ethics	Is more just	Is unfair
Ethics	Increases happiness	Is based on amoral self-interest Is atomistic
Human nature and Ethics	More religious tolerance Sexism and racism decline Peace	Is dog-eat-dog
Human nature	Lessens government corruption	Underestimates human depravity
Epistemology	Is therefore actually best	Is merely a subjective narrative

The next steps are up to you. Happy and productive thinking.

Notes

1 I use *liberal* philosophically and not journalistically to report how it is used in different parts of the world. Language evolves, sometimes for peculiarly local or tendentiously ideological reasons. When a term strays from its cognitive roots, it is important to clarify and re-establish its useful meaning.

2 J. S. Mill, *On Liberty*, 1859, Chapter 2, "Of the Liberty of Thought and Discussion."

3 Aristotle holds: "It is the mark of a free man not to live at another's beck and call"; see *Rhetoric*, c. 350 BCE, 1367a30.

John Locke says about freedom of choice: "We naturally, as I said, even from our cradles, love liberty, and have therefore an aversion to many things, for no other reason, but because they are enjoin'd us"; see *Some Thoughts concerning Education*, 1690, Section 148.

John Stuart Mill says about freedom of movement: "Many a person remains in the same town, street, or house from January to December, without a wish or thought tending towards removal, who, if confined to that same place by the mandate of authority, would find the imprisonment absolutely intolerable"; see *Principles of Political Economy*, 1848, p. 213.

Ayn Rand maintains: "for every individual, a right is the moral sanction of a positive—of his freedom to act on his own judgment, for his own goals, by his own voluntary, uncoerced choice"; see "Man's Rights," 1963, in *The Virtue of Selfishness*, p. 93.

4 Adam Smith says this about the self-interested profit motive leading to mutually-beneficial trade: "It is not from the benevolence of the butcher, the brewer, or the baker that we expect our dinner, but from their regard to their own interest. We address ourselves, not to their humanity but to their self-love." (*On the Wealth of Nations*, 1776, I.2.2).

Alexis de Tocqueville, in his 1830s travel through the young United States, contrasted fields and buildings on the Ohio and Kentucky sides of the Ohio River. Ohio was a free state and Kentucky was a slave state. The Ohio fields were better cultivated, and the structures were built more quickly and of higher quality than those on the Kentucky side. For the Ohio farmers and the hired contractors and laborers, self-interested profit seeking was incentivized. Kentucky's slaves, by contrast, had no liberty rights, no property rights, and no profit motive. (*Democracy in America*, 1835, 1.18.4).

Milton Friedman compares the profit motive to compulsion: "Given sufficient knowledge, it might be that compulsion could be substituted for the incentive of reward, though I doubt that it could. One can shuffle inanimate objects around; one can compel individuals to be at certain places at certain times; but one can hardly compel individuals to put forward their best efforts. Put another way, the substitution of compulsion for co-operation changes the amount of resources available." (*Capitalism and Freedom*, University of Chicago Press, 1962, p. 166).

5   J. S. Mill: "Since European life assumed a settled aspect, anything above mediocrity in a hereditary king has become extremely rare, while the general level has been even below mediocrity, both in talent and in vigour of character." ("Of the Infirmities and Dangers to which Representative Government is Liable", 1861, Chapter 6 of *Essays on Politics and Society*, edited by J. M. Robson, University of Toronto Press, 1977, p. 437.)

6   Friedrich Hayek says this about the epistemic basis of the liberal individualist position: "It merely starts from the indisputable fact that the limits of our powers of imagination make it impossible to include in our scale of values more than a sector of the needs of our whole society, and that, strictly speaking, scales of values can exist only in individual minds, nothing but partial scales of values exist—scales which are inevitably different and often inconsistent with each other. From this the individualist concludes that the individuals should be allowed, within defined limits, to follow their own values and preferences rather than somebody else's; that within these spheres the individual's system of ends should be supreme and not subject to any dictation by others. It is this recognition of the individual as the ultimate judge of his own ends, the belief that as far as possible his own views ought to govern his actions, that forms the essence of the individualist position." See *The Road to Serfdom*, 1944, p. 59.

7   An early version of this point is Adam Smith's identifications of the division of labor into specialties and the coordination of that specialized labor by the "invisible hand" of the market. "The greatest improvements in the productive powers of labour, and the greater part of the skill, dexterity, and judgment with which it is any where directed, or applied, seem to have been the effects of the division of labour." See *Wealth of Nations*, I.1. The coordinating invisible hand line

appears in *Wealth of Nations*, IV.2.

Hayek explicates Smith's metaphor of the invisible hand, in part, in terms of the price system as a signaling mechanism enabling market participants to know best how to use resources: "The price system is just one of those formations which man has learned to use (though he is still very far from having learned to make the best use of it) after he had stumbled upon it without understanding it. Through it not only a division of labor but also a coördinated utilization of resources based on an equally divided knowledge has become possible." See "The Use of Knowledge in Society," *American Economic* Review, 1945, Vol. XXXV, No. 4, pp. 519-530.

8   Mill: "the same reasons which show that opinion should be free, prove also that he should be allowed, without molestation, to carry his opinions into practice at his own cost. That mankind are not infallible; that their truths, for the most part, are only half-truths; that unity of opinion, unless resulting from the fullest and freest comparison of opposite opinions, is not desirable, and diversity not an evil, but a good, until mankind are much more capable than at present of recognizing all sides of the truth, are principles applicable to men's modes of action, not less than to their opinions. As it is useful that while mankind are imperfect there should be different opinions, so is it that there should be different experiments of living; that free scope should be given to varieties of character, short of injury to others; and that the worth of different modes of life should be proved practically, when any one thinks fit to try them." See "Of Individuality, as One of the Elements of Well-Being," Chapter 3 of *On Liberty*, 1859.

9   This is Joseph Schumpeter's thesis of "the perennial gale of creative destruction" as presented in Chapter 7 of *Capitalism, Democracy, and Socialism*, 1950, pp. 83-84.

Professors Yuriy Gorodnichenko and Gerard Roland: "We construct an endogenous growth model that includes a cultural variable along the dimension of individualism-collectivism. The model predicts that more individualism leads to more innovation because of the social rewards associated with innovation in an individualist culture." ("Culture, Institutions and the Wealth of Nations," <a href="http://www.nber.org/papers/w16368">NBER Working Paper No. 16368</a>, September 2010).

10 Ludwig von Mises: "The characteristic feature of modern capitalism is mass production of goods destined for consumption by the masses. The result is a tendency towards a continuous improvement in the average standard of living, a progressing enrichment of the many." (*The Anti-Capitalist Mentality*, p. 1). Mises later notes "the marvelous

achievements of the last two hundred years: the unprecedented improvement of the average standard of living for a continually increasing population" (p. 39). In another work: "Liberalism has always had in view the good of the whole, not that of any special group. It was this that the English utilitarians meant to express—although, it is true, not very aptly—in their famous formula, 'the greatest happiness of the greatest number.' Historically, liberalism was the first political movement that aimed at promoting the welfare of all, not that of special groups." (*Liberalism*, 1927, p. 7).

Schumpeter: "Queen Elizabeth owned silk stockings. The capitalist achievement does not typically consist in providing more silk stockings for queens but in bringing them within reach of factory girls in return for steadily decreasing amounts of effort," (*Capitalism, Democracy, and Socialism*, 1950, p.67)

Economic historian Lawrence White notes that most debates among economists are "not a clash over whose interests the economy should serve, but over how best to foster the prosperity of the economy's average participant"; see *The Clash of Economic Ideas*, Cambridge University Press, 2012, p. 11. Note the word "average" as indicative that this is the standard of value appealed to by most economists.

11 Edmund Phelps notes: "I broadly subscribe to the conception of economic justice in the work by John Rawls", namely that the moral justification of any system is its effect on the least well off. "So if the increased dynamism created by liberating private entrepreneurs and financiers tends to raise productivity, as I argue—and if that in turn pulls up those bottom wages, or at any rate does not lower them—it is not unjust. Does anyone doubt that the past two centuries of commercial innovations have pulled up wage rates at the low end and everywhere else in the distribution?" See "Dynamic Capitalism: Entrepreneurship is lucrative—and just," *The Wall Street Journal*, October 10, 2006.

See also John Tomasi, *Free Market Fairness*, Princeton University Press, 2012.

12 Mises: "It is precisely want and misery that liberalism seems to abolish." "In order to appreciate what liberalism and capitalism have accomplished, one should compare conditions as they are at present with those of the Middle Ages or of the first centuries of the modern era"; see *Liberalism*, pp. 9-10.

13 Tocqueville contrasts the liberal individualism of early America to the long cultural traditions of aristocratic and government patronage in Europe: "Wherever at the head of some new undertaking you see the

government in France, or a man of rank in England, in the United States you will be sure to find an association." Also: "The citizen of the United States is taught from infancy to rely upon his own exertions in order to resist the evils and the difficulties of life ... This habit may be traced even in the schools, where the children in their games are wont to submit to rules which they have themselves established, and to punish misdemeanors which they have themselves defined. The same spirit pervades every act of social life. If a stoppage occurs in a thoroughfare and the circulation of vehicles is hindered, the neighbors immediately form themselves into a deliberative body; and this extemporaneous assembly gives rise to an executive power which remedies the inconvenience before anybody has thought of recurring to a pre-existing authority superior to that of the persons immediately concerned. If some public pleasure is concerned, an association is formed to give more splendor and regularity to the entertainment. Societies are formed to resist evils that are exclusively of a moral nature." (*Democracy in America*, 1:12).

14 Bertrand de Jouvenel argues that a turn away from liberalism would cause the decline of high standards and quality: "The production of all first-quality goods would cease. The skill they demand would be lost and the taste they shape would be coarsened. The production of artistic and intellectual goods would be affected first and foremost. Who could buy paintings? Who even could buy books other than pulp? ... Can we reconcile ourselves to the loss suffered by civilization if creative intellectual and artistic activities fail to find a market?" See *The Ethics of Redistribution*, 1952, pp. 41-42).

15 Mill: "Persons of genius, it is true, are, and are always likely to be, a small minority; but in order to have them, it is necessary to preserve the soil in which they grow. Genius can only breathe freely in an atmosphere of freedom. Persons of genius are, *ex vi termini*, by definition, more individual than any other people." See *On Liberty*, Chapter 3.

16 Thomas Jefferson's formulation in the *Declaration of Independence* (1776) explicitly links life, liberty, and happiness.

Mill: "Where, not the person's own character, but the traditions of customs of other people are the rule of conduct, there is wanting one of the principal ingredients of human happiness." And: "He who lets the world, or his own portion of it, choose his plan of life for him, has no need of any other faculty than the ape-like one of imitation. He who chooses his plan for himself, employs all his faculties. He must use observation to see, reasoning and judgment to foresee, activity to gather materials for decision, discrimination to decide, and when he has decided, firmness and self-control to hold to his deliberate decision." (Chapter 3 of *On Liberty*, 1859).

17 Rand on happiness as self-responsibly earned: "Just as I support my life, neither by robbery nor alms, but by my own effort, so I do not seek to derive my happiness from the injury or the favor of others, but earn it by my own achievement." (*Atlas Shrugged*, 1957, p. 939).

18 Hayek on self-responsibility and success: "Free societies have always been societies in which the belief in individual responsibility has been strong. They have allowed individuals to act on their knowledge and beliefs and have treated the results achieved as due to them. The aim was to make it worth while for people to act rationally and reasonably and to persuade them that what they would achieve depended chiefly on them. This last belief is undoubtedly not entirely correct, but it certainly had a wonderful effect in developing both initiative and circumspection." See "The Moral Element in Free Enterprise," 1962, *Studies in Philosophy, Politics, and Economics*, 1968, p. 232).

19 Mill argues this in *On Liberty*, stressing the dangers of conformity and the benefits of cultivating individuality: "It is not by wearing down into uniformity all that is individual in themselves, but by cultivating it and calling it forth, within the limits imposed by the rights and interests of others, that human beings become a noble and beautiful object of contemplation." And: "it is essential that different persons should be allowed to lead different lives. In proportion as this latitude has been exercised in any age, has that age been noteworthy to posterity." (Chapter 3).

20 Locke on tolerance's basis in individual freedom: "no man can, if he would, conform his faith to the dictates of another. All the life and power of true religion consist in the inward and full persuasion of the mind; and faith is not faith without believing. Whatever profession we make, to whatever outward worship we conform, if we are not fully satisfied in our own mind that the one is true and the other well pleasing unto God, such profession and such practice, far from being any furtherance, are indeed great obstacles to our salvation." (*A Letter concerning Toleration*, 1689).

21 Those cultures historically—classical Athens, Renaissance Florence, the Dutch Golden Age, and others—that encouraged individuality were at the same time cultures with a wider diversity of religion and relative tolerance.

Historic free ports such as Tangier, Beirut, New Orleans, and Hong Kong are further examples of places where individuals from many different nations were at wide liberty to engage in commerce. One significant feature of such ports was the then-rare phenomenon of individuals of different religions trading peacefully with each other, tolerating each other's religious differences, and sometimes even becoming friends.

Also Voltaire on the London Stock Exchange: "Go into the London Stock Exchange—a more respectable place than many a court—and you will see representatives from all nations gathered together for the utility of men. Here Jew, Mohammedan and Christian deal with each other as though they were all of the same faith, and only apply the word infidel to people who go bankrupt. Here the Presbyterian trusts the Anabaptist and the Anglican accepts a promise from the Quaker. On leaving these peaceful assemblies some go to the Synagogue and others for a drink, this one goes to be baptized in a great bath in the name of the Father, Son and Holy Ghost, that one has his son's foreskin cut and has some Hebrew words he doesn't understand mumbled over the child, others go to their church and await the inspiration of God with their hats on, and everybody is happy." (Letter 6, "On Presbyterians," *Letters from England*, 1733).

22 Locke: "This only I say, that, whencesoever their authority be sprung, since it is ecclesiastical, it ought to be confined within the bounds of the Church, nor can it in any manner be extended to civil affairs, because the Church itself is a thing absolutely separate and distinct from the commonwealth. The boundaries on both sides are fixed and immovable. He jumbles heaven and earth together, the things most remote and opposite, who mixes these two societies, which are in their original, end, business, and in everything perfectly distinct and infinitely different from each other." (*A Letter concerning Toleration*, 1689).

The first clause of the First Amendment to the U.S. Constitution: "Congress shall make no law respecting an establishment of religion, or prohibiting the free exercise thereof" (1791).

23 The first anti-slavery societies were in the liberal Enlightenment nations: the American Society for Abolition of Slavery (1784), the British Society for Abolition of Slave Trade (1787), and the French Societé des Amis des Noirs (1788). The first feminist manifestos were Condorcet's essay, "On the Admission of Women to the Rights of Citizenship" (1790), which argued for full equality of rights of women with men, Olympe de Gouges' *The Declaration of the Rights of Woman* (1791), and Mary Wollstonecraft's *A Vindication of the Rights of Women* (1792). All explicitly applied the ideals of the Enlightenment in general and the life, liberty, and pursuit of happiness principles articulated in the U.S. *Declaration of Independence*.

24 Friedman: "The great virtue of a free market system is that it does

not care what color people are; it does not care what their religion is; it only cares whether they can produce something you want to buy. It is the most effective system we have discovered to enable people who hate one another to deal with one another and help one another." ("Why Government Is the Problem," Stanford University, Hoover Institution Press, 1993, p. 19).

25 "The pursuit of commerce reconciles nations, calms wars, strengthens peace, and commutes the private good of individuals into the common benefit of all" (Hugh of Saint Victor, 1096-1141). "Just as war is the natural consequence of monopoly, peace is the natural consequence of freedom." (Gustave de Molinari). Mill: "It is commerce which is rapidly rendering war obsolete, by strengthening and multiplying the personal interests which are in natural opposition to it." (*Principles of Political Economy*, Book III, Chapter XVII, Section 14). Steven Pinker: "The theory of the Liberal Peace embraces as well the doctrine of gentle commerce, according to which trade is a form of reciprocal altruism which offers positive-sum benefits for both parties and gives each a selfish stake in the well-being of the other." (*The Better Angels of Our Nature*, Penguin Books, 2011). The Liberal or Capitalist Peace thesis is sometimes casually called the "No two countries with a McDonald's have ever gone to war" theory.

26 Mises: "The notion of justice makes sense only when referring to a definite system of norms which in itself is assumed to be uncontested and safe against any criticism." (*Human Action*, 1949, p. 720).

27 Rand: "one must never seek or grant the unearned and undeserved, neither in matter nor in spirit (which is the virtue of Justice)." ("The Objectivist Ethics," 1961, *The Virtue of Selfishness*, 1964, p. 28.]

28 Smith: "The most sacred laws of justice, therefore, those whose violation seems to call loudest for vengeance and punishment, are the laws which guard the life and person of our neighbour; the next are those which guard his property and possessions; and last of all come those which guard what are called his personal rights, or what is due to him from the promises of others." (*Theory of Moral Sentiments, 1759*, II.ii.2.3).

29 Locke: "The legislative, or supreme authority, cannot assume to its self a power to rule by extemporary arbitrary decrees, but is bound to dispense justice, and decide the rights of the subject by promulgated standing laws, and known authorized judges: for the law of nature being unwritten, and so no where to be found but in the minds of men, they who through passion or interest shall miscite, or misapply it." (*Second Treatise of Government*, 1689, Section 136).

30 Democide is the killing of citizens by their own government. For the twentieth-century death count, see R. J. Rummel, *Death by Government* (Transaction Publishing, 1993) and updated numbers.

31 Marilyn vos Savant, "Ask Marilyn," *Parade*. 1991.

32 John Maynard Keynes: "It is *not* a correct deduction from the principles of economics that enlightened self-interest always operates in the public interest. Nor is it true that self-interest generally *is* enlightened; more often individuals acting separately to promote their own ends are too ignorant or too weak to attain even these"; see *The End of Laissez-Faire*, 1926.

33 Richard Thaler and Cass Sunstein argue that government regulations can help people by "framing" their decision-making: "Framing works because people tend to be somewhat mindless, passive decision makers. Their Reflective System does not do the work that would be required to check and see whether reframing the questions would produce a different answer. One reason they don't do this is that they wouldn't know what to make of the contradiction. This implies that frames are powerful nudges, and must be selected with caution"; see Richard Thaler and Cass Sunstein, *Nudge: Improving Decisions about Health, Wealth, and Happiness* (Yale University Press, 2008), p. 37.

34 Ortega y Gasset says: "Man, whether he like it or no, is a being forced by his nature to seek some higher authority"; see José Ortega y Gasset, *The Revolt of the Masses* (New York: W. W. Norton & Co., 1932), p. 116.

35 Plato, *Republic*, c. 380 BCE, Book 5, 473d; accessed online at http://classics.mit.edu/Plato/republic.html.

36 Or psychologist-kings—for example, see B. F. Skinner, *Walden Two*, 1948.

37 Joseph de Maistre argues: "Man is so muddled, so dependent on the things immediately before his eyes, that every day even the most submissive believer can be seen to risk the torments of the afterlife for the smallest pleasure." See Joseph de Maistre, "First Dialogue," *Les Soirées de Saint-Pétersbourg* (1821), translated by Richard A. Lebrun. Montreal and Kingston: McGill-Queens University Press, 1993; accessed online at https://openlibrary.org/books/OL1175368M/St._Petersburg_dialogues_or_Conversations_on_the_temporal_government_of_providence.

Also consider this strong version from Fyodor Dostoevsky's Grand Inquisitor: "Freedom, free reason, and science will lead them into such a maze, and confront them with such miracles and insoluble mysteries, that some of them, unruly and ferocious, will exterminate themselves; others, unruly but feeble, will exterminate each other; and the remaining third, feeble and wretched, will crawl to our feet and cry out to us: 'Yes, you were right, you alone possess his mystery, and we are coming back to you—save us from ourselves'" ; see Fyodor Dostoevsky, *The Brothers Karamazov*, 1880, p. 258.

38   Plato, *Republic*, Book 2, 359d-360c.

39   Genesis 3.6.

40   Genesis 4.8.

41   Genesis 6.11.

42   Lord Acton: "All power tends to corrupt, and absolute power corrupts absolutely." Letter to Creighton, April 5, 1887; ; accessed online at "http://oll.libertyfund.org/quote/214.

43   Joseph de Maistre: "Man in general, if reduced to himself, is too wicked to be free. ... He is a monstrous centaur, born of some unimaginable offence, some abominable miscegenation."

Genghis Khan: "The greatest joy a man can know is to conquer his enemies and drive them before him. To ride their horses and take away their possessions, to see the faces of those who were dear to them bedewed with tears, and to clasp their wives and daughters in his arms." (Quoted in Steven Dutch, "The Mongols," 1998; accessed online at http://www.uwgb.edu/dutchs/WestTech/xmongol.htm).

Sigmund Freud: "Men are not gentle creatures who want to be loved, and who at the most can defend themselves if they are attacked; they are, on the contrary, creatures among whose instinctual endowments is to be reckoned a powerful share of aggressiveness. As a result, their neighbor is for them not only a potential helper or sexual object, but also someone who tempts them to satisfy their aggressiveness on him, to exploit his capacity for work without compensation, to use him sexually without his consent, to seize his possessions, to humiliate him, to cause him pain, to torture and kill him. *Homo homini lupus*"; see Sigmund Freud, *Civilization and Its Discontents* (New York: W.W. Norton, 1930), p. 58.

Alexander Solzhenitsyn claims: "Destructive and irresponsible freedom has been granted boundless space. Society has turned out to have scarce defense against the abyss of human decadence, for example against the misuse of liberty for moral violence against young people, such as motion pictures full of pornography, crime, and horror"; see Alexander Solzhenitsyn, "A World Split Apart," 1978, commencement address delivered at Harvard University; accessed online at http://www.americanrhetoric.com/speeches/alexandersolzhenitsynharvard.htm.

Robert Bork argues that "Because both libertarians and modern liberals are oblivious to social reality, both demand radical personal autonomy in expression. That is one reason libertarians are not to be confused, as they often are, with conservatives." "Free market economists are particularly vulnerable to the libertarian virus" because too often the free market economist "ignores the question of which wants it is moral to satisfy" and fails to recognize that "unconstrained human nature will seek degeneracy often enough to create a disorderly, hedonistic, and dangerous society"; see Robert Bork, *Slouching Towards Gomorrah* (New York: Harper Perennial, 1996), pp. 150, 151, 153.

William Golding: "The desire to squeeze and hurt was over-mastering"; see William Golding, *Lord of the Flies*, 1954, Chapter 7.

John Gray states that "Cruelty and conflict are basic human traits"; see John Gray, "The Truth about Evil," *The Guardian*, October 21, 2014; accessed online at http://www.theguardian.com/news/2014/oct/21/-sp-the-truth-about-evil-john-gray.

44 Immanuel Kant says that "the history of freedom begins with *badness*, for it is *man's* work"; see Immanuel Kant, "Speculative Beginning of Human History," 1786, in *Perpetual Peace and Other Essays*, translated by Ted Humphrey (Indianapolis: Hackett, 1983), p. 54.

45 Proverbs 9:10.

René Descartes suggests: "And since in this life one frequently finds greater rewards offered for vice than for virtue, few persons would prefer the just to the useful if they were not restrained either by the fear of God or by the expectation of another life"; see René Descartes, "Letter of Dedication" to *Meditations* [1641], second paragraph; accessed online at: https://en.wikisource.org/wiki/Meditations_on_First_Philosophy/Letter_of_Dedication.

46 Leo Strauss argues that "Because mankind is intrinsically wicked, he has to be governed"; see Leo Strauss, *Natural Right and History* (Chicago: University of Chicago Press, 1965).

47 Solzhenitsyn claims: "I have come to understand the truth of all the religions of the world: They struggle with the *evil inside a human being* (inside every human being). It is impossible to expel evil from the world in its entirety, but it is possible to constrict it within each person"; see Alexander Solzhenitsyn, *The Gulag Archipelago, 1918-1956*

Notes

(New York: Harper & Row, 1973).

48 1 Timothy 6:10.

49 1 Corinthians 7.

50 Matthew 18:21-22.

51 Ortega y Gasset say this about how liberalism has created the mass man: "at the center of his scheme of life there is precisely the aspiration to live without conforming to any moral code." And: "The mass-man is simply without morality, which is always, in essence, a sentiment of submission to something, a consciousness of service and obligation" see *Revolt of the Masses*, pp. 187, 189.

52 Plato: "The first and highest form of the state and of the government and of the law [is a condition] in which the private and individual is altogether banished from life, and things which are by nature private, such as eyes and ears and hands, have become common, and in some way see and hear and act in common, and all men express praise and blame and feel joy and sorrow on the same occasions, and whatever laws there are unite the city to the utmost." (*Laws*, c. 360 BCE, 739 C-D).

53 Professor W. G. Maclagan insists that "a man may and should discount altogether his own pleasure or happiness as such when he is deciding what course of action to pursue." See "Self and Others: A Defense of Altruism," *Philosophical Quarterly* 4 (1954), pp. 109-110.

Solzhenitsyn on the moral superiority of suffering as exemplified by the Russian experience: "Through deep suffering, people in our own country have now achieved a spiritual development of such intensity that the Western system in its present state of spiritual exhaustion does not look attractive." ("A World Split Apart," 1978).

Mother Teresa: "I think it is very beautiful for the poor to accept their lot, to share it with the passion of Christ. I think the world is being much helped by the suffering of the poor people." (Quoted in Robert White, *The Diabolical Works of Mother Teresa*, 2001).

Ludwig Wittgenstein: "I don't know why we are here, but I'm pretty sure that it is not in order to enjoy ourselves;" accessed online at http://www.bbc.co.uk/radio4/history/inourtime/greatest_philosopher_ludwig_wittgenstein.shtml.

54 G. W. F. Hegel: "A single person, I need hardly say, is something subordinate, and as such he must dedicate himself to the ethical whole. Hence, if the state claims life, the individual must surrender

it." (*Philosophy of Right*, 1835).

55 Iris Murdoch: "In the moral life the enemy is the fat, relentless ego." (*The Sovereignty of Good*, Routledge & Kegan Paul, 1970, p. 52).

Johann Gottlieb Fichte: "There is only one virtue—to forget one's own person, and only one vice—to think of oneself"; quoted in Edward Westermarck, *Ethical Relativity* [1932] (London: Routledge, 2010), p. 22).

Arthur Schopenhauer: "In war we must first recognize the enemy; in the impending struggle, *egoism*, as the chief force on its own side, will be the principal opponent of the virtue of *justice*, which, in my opinion, is the first and really cardinal virtue"; see *On the Basis of Morality* [1839] (Indianapolis: Hackett, 1995), p. 134.

John Rawls: "The idea of justice expressed in the political theories of Hobbes and Locke, the view of Adam Smith that we best serve our fellow-men by enlightened self interest, are all false views of community. Any society which explains itself in terms of mutual egoism is heading for certain destruction"; see John Rawls, *A Brief Inquiry into the Meaning of Sin and Faith: With "On My Religion"*, edited by Thomas Nagel (Cambridge: Harvard University Press, 2010).

56 Amartya Sen: "The self-interest view of rationality involves *inter alia* a firm rejection of the 'ethics-related' view of motivation"; see *On Ethics and Economics* (London: Blackwell, 1987), p. 15.

57 Kant: "Now an action done from duty must wholly exclude the influence of inclination and with it every object of the will, so that nothing remains which can determine the will except objectively the law, and subjectively pure respect for this practical law, and consequently the maxim that I should follow this law even to the thwarting of all my inclinations"; see *Groundwork of the Metaphysics of Morals* [1785], translated by H. J. Paton (New York: Harper & Row), section 397.

58 Kant: "the concepts of pleasure and pain, of the desires and inclinations, etc., all of which are of empirical origin, yet in the construction of a system of pure morality these empirical concepts must necessarily be brought into the concept of duty, as representing either a hindrance which we have to overcome, or an allurement, which must not be made into a motive"; see *Critique of Pure Reason* [1781/1787], translated by Norman Kemp Smith, A15/B29.

59 Adam Smith: "The wise and virtuous man is at all times willing that his own private interest should be sacrificed to the public interest of

his own particular order or society. He is at all times willing, too, that the interest of this order or society should be sacrificed to the greater interest of the state or sovereignty, of which it is only a subordinate part. He should, therefore, be equally willing that all those inferior interests should be sacrificed to the greater interest of the universe, to the interest of that great society of all sensible and intelligent beings, of which God himself is the immediate administrator and director." (*The Theory of Moral Sentiments* [1759] (Indianapolis: Liberty Classics, 1976), VI.2.3, p. 384.

Professor Alfred Rocco: "the necessity, for which the older doctrines make little allowance, of sacrifice, even up to the total immolation of individuals, in behalf of society. ... For Liberalism, the individual is the end and society the means; nor is it conceivable that the individual, considered in the dignity of an ultimate finality, be lowered to mere instrumentality. For Fascism, society is the end, individuals the means, and its whole life consists in using individuals as instruments for its social ends"; see "The Political Doctrine of Fascism," 1925.

60 C. S. Lewis: "Men have differed as regards what people you ought to be unselfish to—whether it was only your own family, or your fellow countrymen, or everyone. But they have always agreed that you ought not to put yourself first"; see *Mere Christianity* (Collier, 1952), p. 5.

61 Russell Kirk: In liberal society, man becomes "a social atom, starved for most emotions except envy and ennui, severed from true family-life and reduced to mere household-life, his old landmarks buried, his old faiths dissipated." (*The Conservative Mind*, 1953).

62 Wendell Berry: "I believe that the community—the fullest sense: a place and all its creatures—is the smallest unit of health and that to speak of the health of an isolated individual is a contradiction in family or community or in a destroyed or poisoned ecosystem." (*The Utne Reader*, September-October 1995, p. 61).

63 A nation is a "family writ large," and its language, culture, and history constitute the individual's core identity (Johann Herder, *Ideas for a Philosophy of the History of Mankind*, 1784-91).

64 Fichte: "the individual life has no real existence, since it has no value of itself, but must and *should* sink to nothing; while, on the contrary, the Race alone exists, since it alone *ought to be* looked upon as really living." (*The Characteristics of the Present Age*, 1806).

65 Solzhenitsyn: "The West has finally achieved the rights of man, and even excess, but man's sense of responsibility to God and society has grown dimmer and dimmer. In the past decades, the legalistic

selfishness of the Western approach to the world has reached its peak and the world has found itself in a harsh spiritual crisis and a political impasse." ("A World Torn Apart," 1978).

66 Pope Paul VI against "philosophical liberalism," which is at its "very root an erroneous affirmation of the autonomy of the individual in his activity, his motivation and the exercise of his liberty." See "Apostolic Letter," **1971, on the 80th anniversary of** *Rerum Novarum*, accessed online at http://www.ewtn.com/library/papaldoc/p6oct.htm.

67 F. H. Bradley: The child "is born not into a desert, but into a living world, a whole which has a true individuality of its own, and into a system and order which it is difficult to look at as anything else than an organism, and which even in England, we are now beginning to call by that name." Consequently: "What is it then that I am to realize? We have said it in 'my station and its duties.' To know what a man is ... you must not take him in isolation. He is one of a people, he was born in a family, he lives in a certain society, in a certain state. What he has to do depends on what his place is, what his function is, and that all comes from his station in the organism." ("My Station and Its Duties,"*Ethical Studies*, London: Henry S. King & Co., 1876, p. 155).

68 Edward Sapir: "No two languages are ever sufficiently similar to be considered as representing the same social reality. The worlds in which different societies live are distinct worlds, not merely the same world with different labels attached." ("The Status of Linguistics as a Science," 1929, *Language* Vol. 5, No. 4, p. 207).

Herder's philosophy of language: "A language, then, is the criterion by means of which a group's identity as a homogeneous unit can be established. Without its own language, a *Volk* is an absurdity (*Unding*)." (F. M. Barnard *Herder's Social and Political Thought: From Enlightenment to Nationalism*, Oxford: Clarendon Press, 1965, p. 57).

69 Alasdair MacIntyre: "We all approach our own circumstances as bearers of a particular social identity. I am someone's son or daughter, someone else's cousin or uncle; I am citizen of this or that city ... Hence what is good for me has to be good for one who inhabits these roles. As such, I inherit from the past of my family, my city, my tribe, my nation, a variety of debts, inheritances, rightful expectations and obligations. These constitute the given of my life, my moral starting point. ... This thought is likely to appear alien and even surprising from the standpoint of modern individualism." (*After Virtue*, University of Notre Dame Press, 1981, p. 220).

Charles Taylor: we must reject the liberal view that "men are self-sufficient outside of society." ("Atomism," in *Philosophy and the Human*

Notes

Sciences: Philosophical Papers 2, Cambridge University Press, 1985).

70   Jean-Jacques Rousseau: "Each of us puts his person and all his power in common under the supreme direction of the general will, and, in our corporate capacity, we receive each member as an indivisible part of the whole." (*The Social Contract*, 1762).

71   Karl Marx, "My *own existence* is a social activity. For this reason, what I myself produce I produce for society, and with the consciousness of acting as a social being." (*Economic and Philosophical Manuscripts*, 1844).

72   Hegel: The State is "an absolute unmoved end in itself" and "has supreme right against the individual, whose supreme duty is to be a member of the state." (*Philosophy of Right*).

73   Dostoevsky's Grand Inquisitor: "this need for *communality* of worship is the chief torment of each man individually, and of mankind as a whole, from the beginning of the ages." (*The Brothers Karamazov*, p. 254).

74   John Dewey on real community as consensus: "Individuals do not even compose a social group because they all work for a common end. The parts of a machine work with a maximum of cooperativeness for a common result, but they do not form a community. If, however, they were all cognizant of the common end and all interested in it so that they regulated their specific activity in view of it, then they would form a community." (*Democracy in Education*, 1916).

75   Kant: "To behold virtue in her proper shape is nothing other than to show morality stripped of all admixture with the sensuous and of all the spurious adornments of reward or self-love." (*Groundwork of the Metaphysic of Morals*, 426, footnote).

76   William Wordsworth:

The world is too much with us; late and soon

Getting and spending, we lay waste our powers.

("The World Is Too Much With Us," c. 1802).

77   Gresham's Law: Bad money drives out good.

78   Professor Robert Heilbroner: "If I were asked to name the deadliest subversive force within capitalism—the single greatest source of its waning morality—I would without hesitation name advertising."

79   Professor John Kenneth Galbraith on advertising's "dependence

effect": "If the individual's wants are to be urgent they must be original with himself. They cannot be urgent if they must be contrived for him. And above all they must not be contrived by the process of production by which they are satisfied. For this means that the whole case for the urgency of production, based on the urgency of wants, falls to the ground. One cannot defend production as satisfying wants if that production creates the wants." (*The Affluent Society*, 1958).

80 C. S. Lewis argues that if we imagined a truly Christian society, we would see that "its economic life was very socialistic." And in such a society, "there will be no manufacture of silly luxury items and then even sillier advertisements to persuade us to buy them." ("Social Morality," *Mere Christianity*, Book 3, Chapter 3, Collier, 1943).

81 Irving Kristol, "godfather" of neo-conservatism: "The inner spiritual chaos of the times, so powerfully created by the dynamics of capitalism itself, is such as to make nihilism an easy temptation. A 'free society' in Hayek's sense gives birth in massive numbers to 'free spirits'—emptied of moral substance." (*Capitalism Today*, 1971, p. 13).

82 Solzhenitsyn: "the human soul longs for things higher, warmer, and purer than those offered by today's mass living habits, introduced as by a calling card by the revolting invasion of commercial advertising, by TV stupor, and by intolerable music." ("A World Split Apart," 1978).

83 Ortega y Gasset on modern Europe: "She has adopted blindly a culture which is magnificent, but has no roots." (*Revolt of the Masses*, p. 189).

84 Professor Amitai Etzioni's left-communitarian version: "Man and woman do not live by bread alone; it is unwise to believe that all we need is economic rehabilitation. We require our daily acts to be placed into a context of transcendent meaning and their moral import made clear." ("Nation in need of community values," *The London Times*, February 20, 1995).

Russell Kirk's right-conservative version: "The conservative is concerned, first of all, with the regeneration of the spirit and character—with the perennial problem of the inner order of the soul, the restoration of the ethical understanding, and the religious sanction upon which any life worth living is founded. This is conservatism at its highest." (*The Conservative Mind*, 1953).

85 George F. Will, *Statecraft as Soulcraft*, 1984, p. 94.

86 For example, in *My Brother's Keeper: A Memoir and a Message* (2003),

Etzioni argues for a Third Way politics that is neither capitalist or communist but rather more like a "three-legged stool" (p. 372) in which society achieves a balance between the state (the public sector), the market (the private sector), and the community (the social sector).

87 Miguel de Unamuno, in *The Tragic Sense of Life* (1913): "A human soul is worth all the universe, someone—I know not whom—has said and said magnificently. A human soul, mind you! Not a human life. Not this life. And it happens that the less a man believes in the soul—that is to say in his conscious immortality, personal and concrete—the more he will exaggerate the worth of this poor transitory life. This is the source from which springs all that effeminate, sentimental ebullition against war."

88 "Love not the world, neither the things that are in the world. If any man love the world, the love of the Father is not in him. For all that is in the world, the lust of the flesh, and the lust of the eyes, and the pride of life, is not of the Father, but is of the world." (I John 2:15-16).

89 Jain monks renounce worldly life in its entirety and embrace a rigorously ascetic life, often to the point of not wearing clothing no matter what the weather. A Hindu monk is forbidden having personal possessions or touching money or other valuables, maintaining personal relationships, eating food for pleasure, and sexual contact with women or looking or even thinking about them.

90 "You cannot serve God and money. Therefore, I tell you, do not worry about life, wondering what you will have to eat or drink, or about what you will have to wear." (Matthew 6:24).

91 "It is these who have not defiled themselves with women, for they are chaste; it is these who follow the Lamb wherever he goes; these have been redeemed from mankind as first fruits for God and the Lamb." (Revelation 14:4).

Eastern Orthodox Archpriest Avvakum: "A woman came to confess to me, burdened with many sins, guilty of fornication and all of the sins of the flesh, and, weeping, she began to acquaint me with them all, leaving nothing out, standing before the Gospels. And I, thrice accursed, fell sick myself. I inwardly burned with a lecherous fire, and that hour was bitter to me. I lit three candles and fixed them to the lectern and placed my right hand in the flame, and held it there till the evil passion was burned out, and when I had dismissed the young woman and laid away my vestments, I prayed and went to my house, grievously humbled in spirit." (Quoted in Robert K. Massie, *Peter the Great*, Random, 1980, p. 62).

92 Solzhenitsyn's answer to the question, "What about the main thing in life?" "Live with a steady superiority over life—don't be afraid of misfortune, and do not yearn for happiness." *(The Gulag Archipelago 1918-1956,* 1973).

93 Seyyid Qutb on martyrdom: "When Islam strives for peace, its objective is not that superficial peace which requires that only that part of the earth where the followers of Islam are residing remain secure. The peace which Islam desires is that the religion (i.e., the Law of the society) be purified for God, that the obedience of all people be for God alone." Further: "The highest form of triumph is the victory of soul over matter, the victory of belief over pain, and the victory of faith over persecution." And finally: "All men die, and of various causes, but not all gain such victory. It is God's choosing and honoring a group of people who share death with the rest of mankind but who are singled out from other people for honor." (*Milestones*, 1964, pp. 63, 151).

94 Jean-François Lyotard: "The experience of the human subject—individual and collective—and the aura that surrounds this experience, are being dissolved into the calculation of profitability, the satisfaction of needs, self-affirmation through success. Even the virtually theological depth of the worker's condition, and of work, that marked the socialist and union movements for over a century, is becoming devalorized, as work becomes a control and manipulation of information. These observations are banal." ("The Sublime and the Avant-Garde," in *The Inhuman: Reflections on Time*, translated by Geoffrey Bennington and Rachel Bowlby, Stanford University Press, 1991, pp. 89-107).

95 Solzhenitsyn: "There is no open violence, as in the East; however, a selection dictated by fashion and the need to accommodate mass standards frequently prevents the most independent-minded persons from contributing to public life and gives rise to dangerous herd instincts that block dangerous herd development." ("A World Split Apart").

96 Friedrich Nietzsche on the "last men":

"'What is love? What is creation? What is longing? What is a star?' thus asks the last man, and he blinks.

"The earth has become small, and on it hops the last man, who makes everything small. His race is as ineradicable as the flea-beetle; the last man lives longest.

"'We have invented happiness,' say the last men, and they blink." (*Thus*

Spake Zarathustra, 1883, Preface: 5).

97 Carl Schmitt: "aspiring to a life without political risk (definition of the bourgeois)." (*The Concept of the Political*, 1927, translated by George Schwab, University of Chicago Press, 1996, p. 51, n. 22).

98 Dostoevsky's Grand Inquisitor: "Without a firm idea of what he lives for, man will not consent to live and will sooner destroy himself than remain on earth, even if there is bread all around him." (*The Brothers Karamazov*, 1880, p. 254).

99 Martin Heidegger stated that the quest for authenticity first requires "the overcoming of the *whole bourgeois essence*." (*Reden* speech of 1934).

100 Hermann Hesse on Buddha's journey: "Siddhartha had spent the night in his house with dancing girls and wine, had acted as if he was superior to them towards the fellow-members of his caste, though this was no longer true, had drunk much wine and gone to bed a long time after midnight, being tired and yet excited, close to weeping and despair, and had for a long time sought to sleep in vain, his heart full of misery which he thought he could not bear any longer, full of a disgust which he felt penetrating his entire body like the lukewarm, repulsive taste of the wine, the just too sweet, dull music, the just too soft smile of the dancing girls, the just too sweet scent of their hair and breasts. But more than by anything else, he was disgusted by himself, by his perfumed hair, by the smell of wine from his mouth, by the flabby tiredness and listlessness of his skin. Like when someone, who has eaten and drunk far too much, vomits it back up again with agonising pain and is nevertheless glad about the relief, thus this sleepless man wished to free himself of these pleasures, these habits and all of this pointless life and himself, in an immense burst of disgust."

So: "Siddhartha had one single goal—to become empty, to become empty of thirst, desire, dreams, pleasure and sorrow—to let the Self die. When all the Self was conquered and dead, when all passions and desires were silent, then at last must awaken, the innermost of Being that is no longer Self—the great secret!" (*Siddhartha*, 1922, p. 14).

101 Clement Greenberg: "Twenty-odd years ago all the ambitious young painters I knew in New York saw abstract art as the only way out. Rightly or wrongly, they could see no other way in which to go in order to say something personal. Therefore new, therefore worth saying. Representational art confronted their ambition with too many occupied positions. But it was not so much representation *per se* that cramped them as it was illusion." ("After Abstract Expressionism," *Art International*, 1962, p. 24).

102 Barnett Newman: "The impulse of modern art is this desire to destroy beauty." ("The Sublime Is Now," *The Tiger's Eye*, 1948, p. 172).

103 Hermann Broch (1886-1951) identifies kitsch as "the evil within the value-system of art." "The maker of kitsch does not create inferior art, he is not an incompetent or a bungler, he cannot be evaluated by aesthetic standards; rather he is ethically depraved, a criminal willing radical evil." (In *Geist and Zeitgeist: The Spirit in an Unspiritual Age, Six Essays by Hermann Broch*, Counterpoint Publishing, 2003).

104 Lyotard on the sublime as an attack on "the metaphysics of capital, which is a technology of time": With the sublime, "the will is defeated. The avant-gardist task remains that of undoing the presumption of the mind with respect to time. The sublime feeling is the name of this privation." ("The Sublime and the Avant-Garde").

105 Werner Sombart's 1915 *Merchants and Heroes* is representative. Sombart was early an admirer of Marx, though he drifted to the right after repeatedly being disappointed when the communist revolution failed to materialize. *Merchants and Heroes* contrasts two types—the merchant (represented in his era by the English) and the hero (represented by the Germans). Merchants are of a lower order: they are calculating, interested in profit, money, and the physical comforts of life. Heroes, by contrast, are of higher historical significance, motivated by the ideal of the great deed and sacrifice for a noble calling. Early in Händler und Helden Sombart explains his purpose: "at issue in this war are the *merchant* and the *hero*, the mercantile and heroic *Weltanschauung*, and the culture that pertains to each. The reason why I am trying, by means of these terms, to isolate a profound and comprehensive antagonism between world-views and experiences of the world is the subject of the following analysis." (*Händler und Helden*, 1915).

106 Schmitt in 1927 on a world without war as one of mere entertainment: "A world in which the possibility of war is utterly eliminated, a completely pacified globe, would be a world without the distinction of friend and enemy and hence a world without politics. It is conceivable that such a world might contain many very interesting antitheses and contrasts, competitions and intrigues of every kind, but there would be not a meaningful antithesis whereby men could be required to sacrifice life, authorized to shed blood, and kill other human beings." (*The Concept of the Political*, translated by George Schwab, University of Chicago Press, 1996, p. 35).

107 Already by 1934, Martin Heidegger was calling the Great War "the *first* world war." (*Reden* speech, 280-281; emphasis added).

108 Nietzsche: "To take the right to new values—that is the most terrible

taking for a carrying and reverent spirit. Indeed, it is preying, and the work of a predatory animal." ("On the Three Metamorphoses," *Thus Spoke Zarathustra* [1883], translated by Adrian Del Caro, Cambridge University Press, 2006, p. 17).

109 Nietzsche: "*War essential.* It is vain rhapsodizing and sentimentality to continue to expect much (even more, to expect a very great deal) from mankind, once it has learned not to wage war. For the time being, we know of no other means to imbue exhausted peoples. as strongly and surely as every great war does, with that raw energy of the battleground, that deep impersonal hatred, that murderous coldbloodedness with a good conscience, that communal, organized ardor in destroying the enemy, that proud indifference to great losses, to one's own existence and to that of one's friends, that muted, earthquakelike convulsion of the soul." (*Human, All too Human: A Book for Free Spirits*, translated by R. J. Hollingdale, Cambridge University Press, 1996, Section 477).

110 In his 1934 essay, *On Pain*, Ernst Jünger "rejects the liberal values of liberty, security, ease, and comfort, and seeks instead the measure of man in the capacity to withstand pain and sacrifice."

George Orwell: Adolf Hitler "knows that human beings *don't* only want comfort ... they want struggle and self-sacrifice, not to mention drums, flags and loyalty parades." And on all of the totalitarians: "However they may be as economic theories, Fascism and Nazism are psychologically far sounder than any hedonistic conception of life. The same is probably true of Stalin's militarized version of Socialism. All three of the great dictators have enhanced their power by imposing intolerable burdens upon their people. Whereas Socialism, and even capitalism in a more grudging way, have said to people 'I offer you a good time,' Hitler has said to them 'I offer you struggle, danger and death,' and as a result a whole nation flings itself at his feet." ("Review of *Mein Kampf* by Adolf Hitler," 1940, https://docs.google.com/file/d/0BzmBhYakPbYtT3k5cDd4Sm1SRUE/view?sle=true), viewed April 20, 2015).

111 Nietzsche: "Here one must think profoundly to the very basis and resist all sentimental weakness: life itself is *essentially* appropriation, injury, conquest of the strange and weak, suppression, severity, obtrusion of peculiar forms, incorporation and at the least, putting it mildest, exploitation—but why should one for ever use precisely these words on which for ages a disparaging purpose has been stamped?" (*Beyond Good and Evil*, 259).

112 Heraclitus: "War is father of all and king of all; and some he manifested as gods, some as men; some he made slaves, some free." (B53). And: "We must know that war [πόλεμος/polemos] is common

to all and strife is justice, and that all things come into being through strife necessarily." (C. 500 BCE, fragments B53 and B80).

113 Millicent Bell: "All unions are doomed to be compromises of dominion and submission." ("The Bostonian Story" *Partisan Review* 2, 1985, 113).

114 Carl von Clausewitz: "Rather than comparing [war] to art we could more accurately compare it to commerce, which is also a conflict of human interests and activities; and it is still closer to politics, which in turn may be considered as a kind of commerce on a larger scale." (*On War*, 1832, Book I, Ch. 3).

CEO Kevin O'Leary: "Business is war. I go out there, I want to kill the competitors. I want to make their lives miserable. I want to steal their market share. I want them to fear me and I want everyone on my team thinking we're going to win." (*The Record*, February 5, 2015, http://www.therecord.com/news-story/5322749--business-is-war-kevin-o-leary-tells-university-of-waterloo-students/, viewed March 28, 2015).

115 Michel Foucault: "All knowledge rests upon injustice; there is no right, not even in the act of knowing, to truth or a foundation for truth; and the instinct for knowledge is malicious (something murderous, opposed to the happiness of mankind)." ("Nietzsche, Genealogy, and History," in *Language, Counter-Memory, Practice: Selected Essays and Interviews*. Cornell University Press, 1980). And: "I am simply a Nietzschean, and I try as far as possible, on a certain number of issues, to see with the help of Nietzsche's texts" (*Foucault Live (Interviews, 1961-1984)*, edited by Sylvère Lotringer, translated by Lysa Hochroth and John Johnston, Semiotext(e), 1989, p. 471).

116 Nietzsche: "people now rave everywhere, even under the guise of science, about coming conditions of society in which 'the exploiting character' is to be absent:—that sounds to my ear as if they promised to invent a mode of life which should refrain from all organic functions." (*Beyond Good and Evil*, 259)

117 Foucault: "power is tolerable only on condition that it mask a substantial part of itself. Its success is proportional to its ability to hide its own mechanisms." (*The History of Sexuality, Volume 1, An Introduction*, translated by Robert Hurley, Random House, 1978, p. 86).

118 Schmitt: "In case of need, the political entity must demand the sacrifice of life. Such a demand is in no way justifiable by the individualism of liberal thought. No consistent individualism can entrust to someone other than to the individual himself the right to dispose of the physical

Notes

life of the individual." (*The Concept of the Political*, 1927/1996, p. 71).

119 Thucydides' rendition of the Athenian delegates' speech to the Spartans: "We have done nothing extraordinary, nothing contrary to human nature in accepting an empire when it was offered to us and then in refusing to give it up. Three very powerful motives prevent us from doing so—security, honour, and self-interest. And we were not the first to act in this way. Far from it. It has always been a rule that the weak should be subject to the strong; and besides, we consider that we are worthy of our power." (*History of the Peloponnesian War*, 431 BCE, translated by Rex Warner, Penguin, 1972, Book 1).

120 Thrasymachus in Plato's *Republic*: "I affirm that the just is nothing else than the advantage of the stronger" (338c).

121 Leo Strauss summarizing Schmitt's view: "because man is by nature evil, he therefore needs *dominion*. But dominion can be established, that is, men can be unified only in a unity against—against other men. Every association of men is necessarily a separation from other men ... the political thus understood is not the constitutive principle of the state, of order, but a condition of the state." (Heinrich Meier, *Carl Schmitt and Leo Strauss: the hidden dialogue*, translated by J. Harvey Lomax, University of Chicago Press, 1995, p. 125.)

122 Machiavelli on whether it is more important for a rule to be feared or loved: "The answer is of course, that it would be best to be both loved and feared. But since the two rarely come together, anyone compelled to choose will find greater security in being feared than in being loved." ("Concerning Cruelty and Clemency, and Whether it is Better to Be Loved than Feared," *The Prince*, written in 1513 and published in 1532, Chapter XVII).

123 Rousseau: "Every man by nature has a right to everything he needs." (*The Social Contract*, 1762, 1.9).

124 Rousseau: "it is obviously contrary to the law of nature, however it may be defined, for a child to command an old man, for an imbecile to lead a wise man, and for a handful of people to gorge themselves on superfluities while the starving multitude lacks necessities." (*Discourse on the Origin and Foundations of Inequality among Men*, 1755, translated by Donald Cress, Hackett, 1992, p. 71).

125 Professor Peter Singer: "if it is in our power to prevent something bad from happening, without thereby sacrificing anything of comparable moral importance, we ought, morally, to do it." ("Famine, Affluence, and Morality," *Philosophy and Public Affairs*, Vol. 1, No. 1, Spring 1972, pp. 229-243).

126 Victor Hugo: "There is always more misery among the lower classes than there is humanity among the rich." (*Les Misérables*, 1862).

127 United Nations: "Whereas recognition of the inherent dignity and of the equal and inalienable rights of all members of the human family is the foundation" and "Everyone has the right to a standard of living adequate for the health and well-being of himself and of his family, including food, clothing, housing and medical care and necessary social services, and the right to security in the event of unemployment, sickness, disability, widowhood, old age or other lack of livelihood in circumstances beyond his control." ("The Universal Declaration of Human Rights," 1948, Preamble and Article 25, Section 1, http://www.un.org/en/documents/udhr/, viewed May 3, 2015.)

128 Professor Michael Harrington: "The basic necessities of life—food, shelter, clothing, education, medical care—are met in my Utopia. I don't care if they are lazy, promiscuous, irreverent, rotten people. No one should have to go hungry or cold—scoundrel or not. And in my Utopia I wouldn't change a single facet of human nature as we now know it." (*Omni*, April, 1988).

129 Karl Marx: "From each according to his ability, to each according to his needs!" (*Critique of the Gotha Program*, 1875).

130 Roger Scruton's conservative version: "That, in my view, is the truth in socialism, the truth of our mutual dependence, and of the need to do what we can to spread the benefits of social membership to those whose own efforts do not suffice to obtain them." (*How to Be a Conservative*, Bloomsbury, 2014).

131 We should here contrast the "Liberalism is materialist" and "Liberal societies are boring" arguments above, which argue that liberal capitalism *oversupplies* people's basic material needs and so makes them fat and unhealthy, unmotivated and lazy.

132 John Rawls: "The duty of fair play stands beside those of fidelity and gratitude as a fundamental moral notion; and like them it implies a constraint on self-interest in particular cases." ("Justice as Fairness," *A Theory of Justice*, Harvard University Press, 1971, Section 3).

133 Thomas Nagel, "Moral Luck," in *Mortal Questions*, Cambridge University Press, 1979, pp. 24-38.

134 Rawls: We should consider "the distribution of natural talents as a common asset." But human beings are "born into different positions." And: "undeserved inequalities call for redress; and since inequalities of birth and natural endowment are undeserved, these inequalities are

to be somehow compensated for." (*A Theory of Justice*, p. 100).

135 Professor Elizabeth Warren: "There is nobody in this country who got rich on his own. Nobody. You built a factory out there? Good for you. But I want to be clear: you moved your goods to market on the roads the rest of us paid for; you hired workers the rest of us paid to educate; you were safe in your factory because of police forces and fire forces that the rest of us paid for. You didn't have to worry that marauding bands would come and seize everything at your factory, and hire someone to protect against this, because of the work the rest of us did."

136 Aristotle on the barrenness of money-lending: "The most hated sort [of wealth acquisition] and with the greatest reason, is usury, which makes a gain out of money itself and not from the natural object of it. For money was intended to be used in exchange but not to increase at interest. And this term interest [*tokos*], which means the birth of money from money is applied to the breeding of money because the offspring resembles the parent. Wherefore of all modes of getting wealth, this is the most unnatural." (*Politics*, c. 350 BCE, 1258b).

Karl Marx quotes Martin Luther: "There is on earth no greater enemy of man, after the Devil, than a gripe-money and usurer, for he wants to be God over all men ... Usury is a great, huge monster, like a werewolf ... And since we break on the wheel and behead highwaymen, murderers, and housebreakers, how much more ought we to break on the wheel and kill ... hunt down, curse, and behead all usurers!" (*Capital: A Critique of Political Economy, Volume 1: The Process of Capitalist Production*, 1867, translated by Samuel Moore and Edward Aveling, Charles H. Kerr & Co., 1916, p. 650).

137 Rawls: "So you were an educated man, yes, but who paid for your education; so you were a good man and upright, yes, but who taught you your good manners and so provided you with good fortune that you did not need to steal; so you were a man of a loving disposition and not like the hard-hearted, yes, but who raised you in a good family, who showed you care and affection when you were young so that you would grow up to appreciate kindness—must you not admit that what you have, you have received? Then be thankful and cease your boasting." (*A Brief Inquiry into the Meaning of Sin and Faith: With 'On My Religion'*, Harvard University Press, 2010).

138 In *Crito*, Socrates rejects his right to escape by having the Law make this argument on behalf of the State: "In the first place did we not bring you into existence? Your father married your mother by our aid and begat you. Say whether you have any objection to urge against those of us who regulate marriage?" None, I should reply. "Or against

those of us who regulate the system of nurture and education of children in which you were trained? Were not the laws, who have the charge of this, right in commanding your father to train you in music and gymnastic?" Right, I should reply. "Well, then, since you were brought into the world and nurtured and educated by us, can you deny in the first place that you are our child and slave, as your fathers were before you?" (Plato, *Crito*, c. 390 BCE, 50d-51d).

139 In theological versions, our entire indebtedness is to God. Augustine: "Why should there be such great glory to a human nature—and this undoubtedly an act of grace, no merit preceding unless it be that those who consider such a question faithfully and soberly might have here a clear manifestation of God's great and sole grace, and this in order that they might understand how they themselves are justified from their sins by the selfsame grace which made it so that the man Christ had no power to sin?" (*Enchiridion on Faith, Hope, and Love*, 420 CE, translated by Albert C. Outler, Chapter 11, Section 36).

140 Professor Kai Neilson: "For contemporary egalitarians, some form of economic equality is central as part of a package with legal, political, and social equalities." (*Equality and Liberty: A Defense of Radical Egalitarianism*, Rowman and Littlefield, 1984, p. 6).

141 Rousseau: "The first person who, having enclosed a plot of land, took it into his head to say *this is mine* and found people simple enough to believe him, was the true founder of civil society. What crimes, wars, murders, what miseries and horrors would the human race have been spared, had someone pulled up the stakes or filled in the ditch and cried out to his fellow man: 'Do not listen to this impostor. You are lost if you forget that the fruits of the earth belong to all and the earth to no one!'" (*Discourse on the Origin of Inequality*, 1755, translated by Donald Cress, Hackett, 1992, Part II, p. 44).

Proudhon: "If I were asked to answer the following question: *What is slavery?* and I should answer in one word, *It is murder*, my meaning would be understood at once. No extended argument would be required to show that the power to take from a man his thought, his will, his personality, is a power of life and death; and that to enslave a man is to kill him. Why, then, to this other question: *What is property!* may I not likewise answer, *It is robbery*, without the certainty of being misunderstood; the second proposition being no other than a transformation of the first." ("What is Property?" Chapter 1, 1840).

142 Rawls: "Social and economic inequalities ... are just only if they result in compensating benefits for everyone, and in particular for the least advantaged members of society." (*A Theory of Justice*, Harvard University Press, 1971, pp. 14-15).

143 For example, the German Social Democrats on the need to equalize the size of businesses: "Private ownership of the means of production can claim protection by society as long as it does not hinder the establishment of social justice. Efficient small and medium sized enterprises are to be strengthened to enable them to prevail in competition with large-scale enterprises." ("Godesberg Program of the SPD," November, 1959, section 6).

144 Michael Harrington, *The Other America: Poverty in the United States*. Macmillan, 1962.

Adam Smith may have been first to identify the phenomenon of relative poverty: "By necessaries I understand not only the commodities which are indispensably necessary for the support of life, but what ever the customs of the country renders it indecent for creditable people, even the lowest order, to be without. A linen shirt, for example, is, strictly speaking, not a necessary of life. The Greeks and Romans lived, I suppose, very comfortably, though they had no linen. But in the present times, through the greater part of Europe, a creditable day-laborer would be ashamed to appear in public without a linen shirt, the want of which would be supposed to denote that disgraceful degree of poverty which, it is presumed, nobody can well fall into, without extreme bad conduct. Custom, in the same manner, has rendered leather shoes a necessary of life in England." (*On the Wealth of Nations*, 1776, V,ii,2).

145 Karl Marx and Friedrich Engels: "The modern bourgeois society that has sprouted from the ruins of feudal society has not done away with class antagonisms. It has but established new classes, new conditions of oppression, new forms of struggle in place of the old ones." (*The Communist Manifesto*, 1848).

146 Rousseau on why comparative advantage and free trade are threats: "It cannot be denied that it is advantageous to have each sort of land produce the things for which it is best suited; by this arrangement you get more out of a country, and with less effort, than in any other way. But this consideration, for all its importance, is only secondary. It is better for the land to produce a little less and for the inhabitants to lead better-regulated lives. With any movement of trade and commerce it is impossible to prevent destructive vices from creeping into a nation." ("Constitutional Project for Corsica," drafted 1765).

147 Joseph Stiglitz: "There are good reasons why plutocrats should care about inequality anyway—even if they're thinking only about themselves. The rich do not exist in a vacuum. They need a functioning society around them to sustain their position. Widely unequal societies do not function efficiently and their economies are neither stable nor

sustainable. The evidence from history and from around the modern world is unequivocal: there comes a point when inequality spirals into economic dysfunction for the whole society, and when it does, even the rich pay a steep price." ("The 1 Percent's Problem," *Vanity Fair*, May 31, 2012, http://www.vanityfair.com/news/2012/05/joseph-stiglitz-the-price-on-inequality , viewed May 11, 2015).

148 David Hume: "Render possessions ever so equal, men's different degrees of art, care, and industry, will immediately break that equality. Or if you check these virtues, you reduce society to the most extreme indigence; and, instead of preventing want and beggary in a few, render it unavoidable to the whole community." ("Of Justice," *An Enquiry concerning the Principles of Morals*, 1751, Part II).

149 Perhaps incorporating various cultures' wise folk sayings: "The nail that sticks up gets hammered down," and "In a field of wheat, only the stalk whose head is empty of grain stands above the rest."

150 Rousseau: "Those who dare to undertake the institution of a people must feel themselves capable, as it were, of changing human nature, of transforming each individual ... into a part of a much greater whole ... of altering the constitution of man for the purpose of strengthening it." (*The Social Contract*, 1762, II.ii.7).

151 Rousseau: "Everyone should make a living, and no one should grow rich; that is the fundamental principle of the prosperity of the nation." (*Constitutional Project for Corsica*, drafted 1765).

152 Richard Rorty argues that social theory must grapple with our "ethnocentric" predicament: "we must, in practice, privilege our own group." Accordingly, "there are lots of views which we simply cannot take seriously." (*Objectivity, Relativism, and Truth*, Cambridge University Press, 1991, p. 29).

153 See Professor Sven Beckert's survey review: "Slavery and Capitalism," *The Chronicle of Higher Education*, December 12, 2014, http://chronicle.com/article/SlaveryCapitalism/150787/.

154 Professor Catharine MacKinnon applies this to speech in a call for government-management: "The law of equality and the law of freedom of speech are on a collision course in this country." (*Only Words*, Harvard University Press, 1993, p. 71).

155 In *The Republic*, Plato has Socrates suggest that to avoid the corruptions that family attachments can cause, the guardian class should institute a communism of women and children (423e-424a).

Religious versions of egalitarianism here cite Jesus's command to

"Love your neighbor as yourself" (Matthew 22:39). Later, someone came up to Jesus when he was conversing with his disciples and said, "Your mother and your brothers are standing outside seeking to speak to you." But Jesus answered and said, "Who is my mother and who are my brothers?" Stretching out his hand toward his disciples, he said, "Behold by mother and my brothers!" (Matthew 12:47-49).

A character in Thomas Hardy's *Jude the Obscure*: "The beggarly question of parentage—what is it, after all? What does it matter, when you come to think of it, whether a child is yours by blood or not? All the little ones of our time are collectively the children of us adults of the time, and entitled to our general care. The excessive regard of parents for their own children, and their dislike of other people's is, like class-feeling, patriotism, save-your-own-soul-ism, and the other virtues, a mean exclusiveness at bottom." (*Jude the Obscure*, 1895, pp. 340-341).

156 Rousseau: "the private will tends by its nature toward preferences and the general will toward equality," so the state "ought to have a universal compulsory force to move and arrange each part in the manner best suited to the whole." (*The Social Contract*, 1762, II.i.3 and II.ii.4).

157 Professors Donella H. Meadows, Dennis L. Meadows, Jørgen Randers, and William W. Behrens III, *The Limits to Growth*, Universe Books, 1972.

158 Thomas Malthus: "Population, when unchecked, goes on doubling itself every 25 years or increases in a geometrical ratio." (*An Essay on the Principle of Population*, 1798, Chapter VII).

159 "Nature, red in tooth and claw." (Alfred Lord Tennyson, *In Memoriam A. H. H.*, 1850, Canto 56.)

160 Charles Darwin: "More individuals are born than can possibly survive. A grain in the balance will determine which individual shall live and which shall die,—which variety or species shall increase in number, and which shall decrease, or finally become extinct." And: "With animals having separated sexes there will in most cases be a struggle between the males for possession of the females. The most vigorous individuals, or those which have most successfully struggled with their conditions of life, will generally leave most progeny." ("Recapitulation," Chapter XIV of *Origin of Species*, 1859). Darwin warned against interpreting *strongest* too mechanically, saying that it is the most *adaptable* that survive: "It is not the strongest of the species that survives, nor the most intelligent, but the most responsive to change."

161 Malthus: "The power of population is so superior to the power of

the earth to produce subsistence for man, that premature death must in some shape or other visit the human race. The vices of mankind are active and able ministers of depopulation. They are the precursors in the great army of destruction, and often finish the dreadful work themselves. But should they fail in this war of extermination, sickly seasons, epidemics, pestilence, and plague advance in terrific array, and sweep off their thousands and tens of thousands. Should success be still incomplete, gigantic inevitable famine stalks in the rear, and with one mighty blow levels the population with the food of the world." (*An Essay on the Principle of Population*, Chapter VII).

162 Nietzsche: "'One furthers one's ego always at the expense of others'; 'Life always lives at the expense of other life'—he who does not grasp this has not taken even the first step toward honesty with himself." (*The Will to Power*, 369).

163 The zero-sum conflict also holds for psychological values: "We acquire glory only to the detriment of others, of those who seek it too, and there is no reputation that is not won at the cost of countless abuses. The man who has emerged from anonymity, or who merely strives to do so, proves that he has eliminated every scruple from his life, that he has triumphed over his conscience, if by some chance he ever had such a thing." (E. M. Cioran, *History and Utopia*, University of Chicago Press, 1998, pp. 65-66).

164 Marx and Engels: Capitalism "has drowned the most heavenly ecstasies of religious fervour, of chivalrous enthusiasm, of Philistine sentimentalism, in the icy water of egotistical calculation. It has resolved personal worth into exchange value, and in place of numberless indefeasible chartered freedoms, it has set up that single, unconscionable freedom—free trade. In one word, for exploitation, veiled by religious and political illusions, it has substituted naked, shameless, direct, brutal exploitation. (Karl Marx and Friedrich Engels, *The Communist Manifesto*, 1848).

165 Herbert Spencer: "This *survival of the fittest*, which I have here sought to express in mechanical terms, is that which Mr. Darwin has called 'natural selection', or the preservation of favoured races in the struggle for life." (*Principles of Biology*, 1864, vol. 1, p. 444).

166 Richard Hofstadter, *Social Darwinism in American Thought, 1860–1915*, University of Pennsylvania Press, 1944.

167 Professor Dale C. Copeland: "leaders are likely to fear a loss of access to raw materials and markets, giving them more incentive to initiate crises to protect their commercial interests." (*Economic Interdependence and War*, Princeton University Press, 2014).

168 Michael Harrington on the socialist vision: "It is the idea of an utterly new society in which some of the fundamental limitations of human existence have been transcended. Its most basic premise is that man's battle with nature has been completely won and there is therefore more than enough of material goods for everyone. As a result of this unprecedented change in the environment, a psychic mutation takes place: invidious competition is no longer programmed into life by the necessity of a struggle for scarce resources; cooperation, fraternity and equality become natural. (*Socialism*, Saturday Review of Books, 1970, p. 344).

169 John Maynard Keynes: "The time has already come when each country needs a considered national policy about what size of population, whether larger or smaller than at present or the same, is most expedient. And having settled this policy, we must take steps to carry it into operation. The time may arrive a little later when the community as a whole must pay attention to the innate quality as well as to the mere numbers of its future members." See *The End of Laissez-Faire*, 1926, Section 4; accessed online at http://www.panarchy.org/keynes/laissezfaire.1926.html.

170 Professor Devon G. Peña: "Since capitalism is inherently expansionist it eventually and inevitably must degrade the environment. This is the second contradiction: Because of its expansionist quality, capitalism inevitably destroys the natural conditions of production (land, water, other resources, and labor)." ("Why Capitalism, Not Population Is Our Greatest Environmental Threat," Alternet, September 24, 2012, http://www.alternet.org/environment/why-capitalism-not-population-our-greatest-environmental-threat, viewed April 17, 2015.)

171 Garrett Hardin, "The Tragedy of the Commons," *Science*, 13 December 1968: Vol. 162, No. 3859, pp. 1243-1248. http://www.sciencemag.org/content/162/3859/1243.full.

172 John Muir: "These temple-destroyers, devotees of ravaging commercialism, seem to have a perfect contempt for Nature, and instead of lifting their eyes to the God of the mountains, lift them to the Almighty Dollar." (*The Yosemite*, 1912, Chapter 15, http://vault.sierraclub.org/john_muir_exhibit/writings/the_yosemite/, viewed April 20, 2015.)

173 Paul Ehrlich: "We must cut out the cancer of population growth. Coercion? Perhaps, but coercion in a good cause." (*The Population Bomb*, Ballantine Publishers, 1968, p. 11).

Professor Paul Taylor: "Given the total, absolute, and final disappearance of Homo Sapiens, not only would the Earth's community of life continue to exist, but in all probability, its well-being would be enhanced. Our presence, in short, is not needed. And if we were to take the standpoint of that Life Community and give voice to its true interests, the ending of the human epoch on Earth would most likely be greeted with a hearty 'Good riddance!'" (*Respect for Nature: A Theory of Environmental Ethics*, Princeton University Press, 2011, p. 115).

174 Professor Razmig Keucheyan: "A world of environmental desolation and conflict will work for capitalism, as long as the conditions for investment and profit are guaranteed. And, for this, good old finance and the military are ready to serve. Building a revolutionary movement that will put a stop to this insane logic is therefore not optional. Because, if the system can survive, it doesn't mean that lives worth living will." ("Not even climate change will kill off capitalism," *The Guardian*, March 6, 2014, http://www.theguardian.com/commentisfree/2014/mar/06/not-even-climate-change-will-kill-off-capitalism, viewed April 17, 2015).

175 E.g., a document prepared for the United Nations Conference on Sustainable Development: "Basic resources and companies should be in the hands of the public sector and society." Further: "sustainable development can only be achieved from a global perspective and cannot be achieved only in the national level." ("End poverty, overcome inequality, save the Earth: Inextricably linked objectives in 2012," January 2012, http://climateandcapitalism.com/2012/01/01/bolivias-proposal-to-rio20-for-the-rights-of-nature/, viewed April 20, 2015).

176 John Maynard Keynes: "Let us clear from the ground the metaphysical or general principles upon which, from time to time, laissez-faire has been founded. It is not true that individuals possess a prescriptive 'natural liberty' in their economic activities. There is no 'compact' conferring perpetual rights on those who Have or on those who Acquire. The world is not so governed from above that private and social interest always coincide. It is not so managed here below that in practice they coincide. It is not a correct deduction from the principles of economics that enlightened self-interest always operates in the public interest. Nor is it true that self-interest generally is enlightened; more often individuals acting separately to promote their own ends are too ignorant or too weak to attain even these. Experience does not show that individuals, when they make up a social unit, are always less clear-sighted than when they act separately." (*The End of Laissez Faire*, 1926).

Notes

177 Keynes: "The most important Agenda of the State relate not to those activities which private individuals are already fulfilling, but to those functions which fall outside the sphere of the individual, to those decisions which are made by no one if the State does not make them. The important thing for government is not to do things which individuals are doing already, and to do them a little better or a little worse; but to do those things which at present are not done at all." (*The End of Laissez Faire*, 1926).

178 Professor Newt Gingrich's right-conservative version, which he calls "opportunity society conservatism": "The opportunity society calls not for a *laissez-faire* society in which the economic world is a neutral jungle of purely random individual behavior, but for forceful government intervention on behalf of growth and opportunity." (*Window of Opportunity: Blueprint for the Future*, Tor Books, 1984).

Nobel-Prize-winning Joseph Stiglitz's left-egalitarian version: "Markets on their own will not do a good job in creating a learning society. Laissez-faire market economies will not succeed. They will not be the most efficient. There need to be systematic interventions by government." ("Mind the Gap," RSA Angus Millar Lecture, *Herald Scotland*, August 31, 2014, http://www.heraldscotland.com/business/company-news/mind-the-gap.25180183, viewed May 3, 2015).

179 Thucydides, *History of the Peloponnesian War*, 2.7.

180 St. Augustine on the sin of intellectual pride by those who learn natural philosophy: "they that know it, exult, and are puffed up; and by an ungodly pride departing from Thee, and failing of Thy light, they foresee a failure of the sun's light, which shall be, so long before, but see not their own, which is." (*Confessions*, 397-400 CE, Book 5, 3.3).

John Calvin: "Our reason is overwhelmed by so many forms of deceptions, is subject to so many errors, dashes against so many obstacles, is caught in so many difficulties, that it is far from directing us aright." (*Institutes of the Christian Religion*, 1536, 2:2:25).

181 Kant on the value of showing reason incapable of knowing reality: "But, above all, there is the inestimable benefit, that all objections to morality and religion will be forever silenced, and this in Socratic fashion, namely, by the clearest proof of the ignorance of the objectors." (*Critique of Pure Reason*, 1781/1787, Bxxxi).

Kierkegaard concludes that faith requires "a crucifixion of the understanding." (*Concluding Unscientific Postscript to Philosophical Fragments*, 1846, translated by H. V. Hong and E. H. Hong, Princeton University

Press, 1992, p. 564).

182 Plato suggests that a society's guardians are justified in noble lies: "The rulers then of the city may, if anybody, fitly lie on account of enemies or citizens for the benefit of the state." (*The Republic*, 389b).

Tocqueville argues that citizens of a democracy need dogmatism in religion even if the religion is not true: "I have laid it down in a preceding chapter that men cannot do without dogmatical belief; and even that it is very much to be desired that such belief should exist amongst them. I now add, that of all the kinds of dogmatical belief the most desirable appears to me to be dogmatical belief in matters of religion." (*Democracy in America*, 1835, "Of the Manner in Which Religion in the United States Avails Itself of Democratic Tendencies," 2.1.5).

Freud is an atheist who is contemptuous of religion—"the whole thing is so patently infantile, so foreign to reality—but he argues that the common man needs religion as he is not sophisticated to seek a meaningful life through the more demanding pursuits of art and science. (*Civilization and Its Discontents*, 1927, Chapter 2).

183 Hume notes wryly about those who make this mistake: "In every system of morality, which I have hitherto met with, I have always remarked, that the author proceeds for some time in the ordinary way of reasoning, and establishes the being of a God, or makes observations concerning human affairs; when of a sudden I am surprized to find, that instead of the usual copulations of propositions, is, and is not, I meet with no proposition that is not connected with an ought, or an ought not." ("Moral Distinctions Not Derived from Reason," *A Treatise of Human Nature*, 1738, 3.1.1).

184 Professor C. L. Stevenson: "'This is good' means *I approve of this; do so as well.*" ("The Emotive Meaning of Ethical Terms," 1937, in A. J. Ayer, editor, *Logical Positivism*, The Free Press, 1959, pp. 264-281).

185 Ludwig Wittgenstein: "Theories which make a proposition of logic appear substantial are always false." (*Tractatus Logico-Philosophicus*, 1922, 6.111).

A. J. Ayer: "The principles of logic and mathematics are true universally simply because we never allow them to be anything else." (*Language, Truth, and Logic*, 1936, Dover edition, p. 77).

186 Heraclitus: "The sea is the purest and the impurest water. Fish can drink it, and it is good for them; to men it is undrinkable and destructive." (Fragments, B61).

Notes

187 Professor N. R. Hanson: "theories and interpretations are 'there' in the seeing from the outset." ("Observation," Chapter 1 of *Patterns of Discovery*, Cambridge University Press, 1958).

Karl Popper: *"there is no sense organ in which anticipatory theories are not genetically incorporated."* And: sense organs "incorporate, more especially, theory-like expectations. Sense organs, such as the eye, are prepared to react to certain selected environmental events—to those events which they 'expect', and *only* to those events. Like theories (and prejudices) they will in general be blind to others: to those which they do not understand, which they cannot interpret (because they do not correspond to any specific problem which the organism is trying to solve.)" (*Objective Knowledge*, Oxford University Press, 1972, pp. 72 and 145).

188 Blaise Pascal: "The heart has its reasons, which reason does not know." (*Pensées*, 1670, 277).

Hume: "Reason is, and ought to be the slave of the passions." (*Treatise*, 2.3.3.4).

Nietzsche: "It is our needs that interpret the world; our drives and their For and Against. Every drive is a kind of lust to rule; each one has its perspective that it would like to compel all the other drives to accept as a norm." (*The Will to Power*, 481).

189 Cass Sunstein: "For the individual agent, rationality is a function of social norms. A norm-free conception of rationality would have to depend on a conception of what peoples' rational 'interests' are in a social vacuum. Since people never act in a social vacuum, such a conception would not be intelligible." (*Free Markets and Social Justice*, Oxford University Press, 1997, p. 54).

Michel Foucault: "I claim that reason is a long narrative, which ends today and makes room for another, and makes no sense." (*Foucault Live*, p. 251).

190 Thomas Kuhn: "We may, to be more precise, have to relinquish the notion, explicit or implicit, that changes of paradigm carry scientists and those who learn from them closer and closer to the truth." (*The Structure of Scientific Revolutions*, University of Chicago Press, 1962, p. 170).

191 Professor Brian Medlin: "it is now pretty generally accepted by professional philosophers that ultimate ethical principles must be arbitrary." ("Ultimate Principles and Ethical Egoism," *Australasian Journal of Philosophy* 35:2. 1957, pp. 111-118).

192 John Calvin: "By predestination we mean the eternal decree of God, by which he determined with himself whatever he wished to happen with regard to every man. All are not created on equal terms, but some are preordained to eternal life, others to eternal damnation; and, accordingly, as each has been created for one or other of these ends, we say that he has been predestinated to life or to death." (*Institutes of the Christian Faith*, 3.21.5).

193 Nietzsche: we are before "a brazen wall of fate; we *are* in prison, we can only *dream* ourselves free, not make ourselves free." (*Human, All-too-Human*, 1878, 2:33). And: "the voluntary is absolutely lacking ... everything has been directed along certain lines from the beginning." (*The Will to Power*, 458).

194 St. Augustine: "What merit, then, has man before grace which could make it possible for him to receive grace, when nothing but grace produces good merit in us; and what else but His gifts does God crown when He crowns our merits? For, just as in the beginning we obtained the mercy of faith, not because we were faithful but that we might become so, in like manner He will crown us at the end with eternal life, as it says, 'with mercy and compassion.' Not in vain, therefore, do we sing to God: 'His mercy shall prevent me,' and 'His mercy shall follow me.' Consequently, eternal life itself, which will certainly be possessed at the end without end, is in a sense awarded to antecedent merits, yet, because the same merits for which it is awarded are not effected by us through our sufficiency, but are effected in us by grace, even this very grace is so called for no other reason than that it is given freely; not, indeed, that it is not given for merit, but because the merits themselves are given for which it is given. And when we find eternal life itself called grace, we have in the same Apostle Paul a magnificent defender of grace: 'The wages of sin,' he says, 'is death. But the grace of God life everlasting in Christ Jesus our Lord.'" (Letter to Sixtus, 418 CE, translated by Sr. Wilfred Parsons, *St. Augustine, Letters*, Volume 4, Catholic University of America Press, 1955).

195 E. O. Wilson: "the question of interest is no longer whether human social behavior is genetically determined; it is to what extent. The accumulated evidence for a large hereditary component is more detailed and compelling than most persons, even geneticists, realize. I will go further; it is already decisive." (*On Human Nature*, Harvard University Press, 1978).

196 Marx: "It is not the consciousness of men that determines their lives, but, on the contrary, their social being that determines their consciousness." (*A Contribution to the Critique of Political Economy*, 1859, Progress Publishers, Moscow, 1977, "Preface").

David Reisman: "Social science has helped us become more aware of the extent to which individuals, great and little, are the creatures of their cultural conditioning; and so we neither blame the little nor exalt the great." (*Individualism Reconsidered*, Doubleday, 1954).

B. F. Skinner: "The illusion that freedom and dignity are respected when control seems incomplete arises in part from the probabilistic nature of operant behavior. Seldom does any environmental condition 'elicit' behavior in the all-or-nothing fashion of a reflex; it simply makes a bit of behavior more likely to occur." (*Beyond Freedom and Dignity*, 1971, Hackett Publishing Company, 2002, pp. 231-232).

197 Marx: "The phantoms formed in the human brain are also, necessarily, sublimates of their material life-process, which is empirically verifiable and bound to material premises. Morality, religion, metaphysics, all the rest of ideology and their corresponding forms of consciousness, thus no longer retain the semblance of independence." (*The German Ideology*, 1845, Part A, Section 1, Part 4).

198 A Stoic is about to beat his slave for an infraction, but the slave is learned about Stoic philosophy and exclaims, "Master, do not punish me for what I did, for I was determined to do it and could not help it!" "Well," replies the master, "then it was determined that I punish you. Stop complaining."

Acknowledgements

I thank the following for thoughtful comments on drafts of the manuscript: Larry Abrams, Carrie-Ann Biondi, Jurgis Brakas, Robert Bradley, John Davis, Michael Davison, Douglas J. Den Uyl, Joshua C. Hall, David R. Henderson, R. Kevin Hill, Shawn E. Klein, Piotr Kostyło, Mohamad Machine-Chian, Terry Noel, Douglas Rasmussen, Sandra Rice, Fred Seddon, Ezequiel Spector, Nathan Tierney, and Leonidas Zelmanovitz.

I thank the following for much-appreciated financial support that made extra writing time possible: Zoltan Cendes, Larry Abrams Charitable Fund, The Stata Foundation, John Kannarr, Joseph Plauché, James Fencil, and the Madden Family Foundation.

About the Author

Stephen R. C. Hicks is Professor of Philosophy at Rockford University, Illinois.

He is author of *Explaining Postmodernism: Skepticism and Socialism from Rousseau to Foucault* (Connor Court, 2019), *Nietzsche and the Nazis* (Ockham's Razor, 2010), and *The Art of Reasoning: Readings for Logical Analysis* (W. W. Norton & Co., 1998), and *Entrepreneurial Living* (CEEF, 2016). He has also published in *Business Ethics Quarterly*, *Review of Metaphysics*, and *The Wall Street Journal*. His writings have been translated into eighteen languages.

He has held visiting positions at Georgetown University in Washington, D.C., the Social Philosophy & Policy Center in Bowling Green, Ohio, Harris Manchester College of Oxford University, England, and the University of Kasimir the Great, Poland.

His website is www.StephenHicks.org.

www.ingramcontent.com/pod-product-compliance
Ingram Content Group UK Ltd.
Pitfield, Milton Keynes, MK11 3LW, UK
UKHW021309180426
11947UKWH00015B/1113